Lessons from Jacob

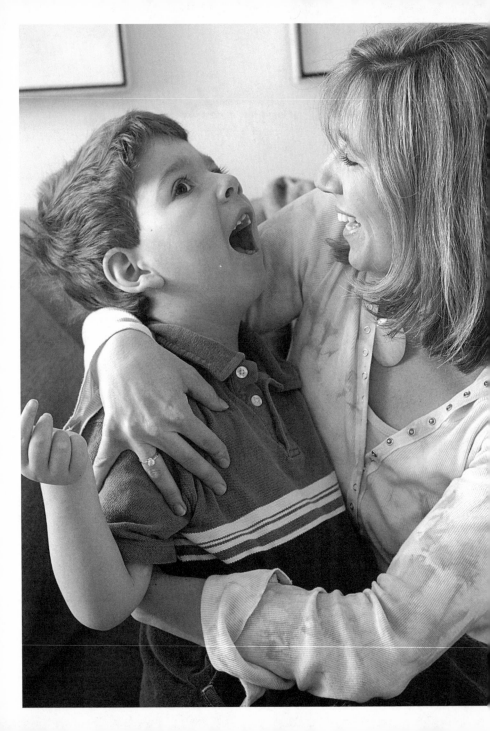

From my heart to yours, Ellen.

Lessons from Jacob

A DISABLED SON TEACHES HIS MOTHER
ABOUT COURAGE, HOPE AND
THE JOY OF LIVING EACH DAY TO THE FULLEST

ELLEN SCHWARTZ

with Edward Trapunski

KEY PORTER BOOKS

Library and Archives Canada Cataloguing in Publication

Schwartz, Ellen (Ellen A.) Lessons from Jacob : A Disabled Son Teaches his Mother about Courage, Hope and the Joy of Living Each Day to the Fullest / Ellen Schwartz with Edward Trapunski.

ISBN 1-55263-850-2

1. Schwartz, Jacob—Health. 2. Canavan disease—Patients—Canada—Biography. I. Trapunski, Edward, 1947– II. Title.

RJ399.C26S34 2006   618.92'830092   C2006-901811-1

THE CANADA COUNCIL | LE CONSEIL DES ARTS
FOR THE ARTS | DU CANADA
SINCE 1957 | DEPUIS 1957

ONTARIO ARTS COUNCIL
CONSEIL DES ARTS DE L'ONTARIO

The publisher gratefully acknowledges the support of the Canada Council for the Arts and the Ontario Arts Council for its publishing program. We acknowledge the support of the Government of Ontario through the Ontario Media Development Corporation's Ontario Book Initiative.

We acknowledge the financial support of the Government of Canada through the Book Publishing Industry Development Program (BPIDP) for our publishing activities.

Partial proceeds from the sale of this book will go to Jacob's Ladder.

Key Porter Books Limited
Six Adelaide Street East, Tenth Floor
Toronto, Ontario
Canada M5C 1H6

www.keyporter.com

Photo credits: all photos courtesy of Ellen Schwartz, except: pp. 2, 136, photos by Kathleen Finlay
Text design: Martin Gould
Electronic formatting: Jean Lightfoot Peters

Printed and bound in Canada

06 07 08 09 10 5 4 3 2 1

For Jeff, Beverly, Ben, and Jacob

Table of Contents

The stewardess comes in and says, "Welcome to Holland."

"Holland?!?" you say. "What do you mean Holland? I signed up for Italy! I'm supposed to be in Italy. All my life I've dreamed of going to Italy."

But there's been a change in the flight plan. They've landed in Holland and there you must stay. So you must go out and buy new guide books. And you must learn a whole new language. And you will meet a whole new group of people you would never have met.

But... if you spend your life mourning the fact that you didn't get to Italy, you may never be free to enjoy the very special, the very lovely things... about Holland.

—Emily Perl Kingsley

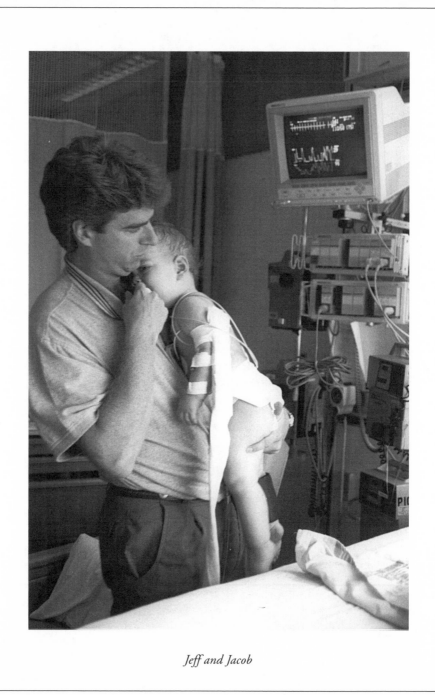

Jeff and Jacob

Introduction

"THERE'S A PROBLEM WITH JACOB."

It was happening, the worst possible nightmare imaginable for a new parent. For any parent.

After the birth of our son—our first child—my husband Jeff and I had been anxiously attentive to any and all signs of Jacob's development. We looked forward to each new sign. But frustratingly, the signs had been slow to develop. Jacob seemed visually inattentive. His eyes would wander without settling anywhere. He seemed indifferent to sounds around him. Should we be worried? I figured we were just fussing over nothing.

We talked with our parents. We consulted friends. We read books. It was probably nothing.

Weeks passed, however, with no improvement. His head tended to loll to one side.

Something was definitely wrong.

I wanted the doctors to reassure me. To tell me that I was over-reacting. Instead, the doctors decided to conduct a series of tests in an attempt to isolate the source of Jacob's "slow" development.

Jacob was two months old.

The tests seemed to go on forever. One after another. Every time more painful and invasive than the one before. It broke our hearts to see Jacob poked and prodded with so many needles. I felt so guilty that I had subjected him to such awful pain.

In September 1997, we were called down to the Hospital for Sick Children in Toronto. Jeff and I had been on tenterhooks for weeks. After so many tests it was exhilarating to know that finally the doctors had news. And more important: a treatment.

Everything was going to be okay. We knew it.

I knew it.

"The good news is we have a diagnosis."

I squeezed Jeff's hands, hopeful.

"The bad news." It was like my heart stopped beating. I tried to swallow but couldn't. I squeezed Jeff's hand harder. "The diagnosis is not a good one. Jacob has Canavan disease."

I stared at her uncomprehendingly.

"It's a rare, inherited, fatal neurodegenerative disorder for which there is no known treatment or cure."

The words flew by in a confused and meaningless chaos.

All I heard was *fatal*.

She must be talking about some other child. Not our child. Not Jacob. No, this couldn't be. She could not possibly be saying what I thought I was hearing. Jeff and I started peppering her with questions.

"Will he speak?"

"No."

"Will he sit up?"

"No."

"Will he go to school?"

"No."

"Will he be able to see?"

"No."

"Will he be able to eat?"

"No."

"Will he ever say 'Mommy' or 'Daddy'?"

"No."

It felt like a huge door had just swung shut on my wonderful dream. How was I to know then that, in fact, I had just been handed a most wonderful miracle.

I REMEMBER LEAVING THE HOSPITAL THAT DAY AND feeling like I had aged fifty years. We were both in a daze. We talked, but nothing seemed real. I remember thinking, "How could I go home and be the mother I had always dreamed of being? How could we watch our son suffer and eventually die? How could I care for him?"

This couldn't be real. This was a mistake. In my anger and grief and self-pity I remember wailing, "Why does this have to happen to me!"

We must be dreaming. It was a nightmare. I just wanted to wake up.

But I never did.

❀ ❀ ❀

Jacob is completely immobile.

He can't feed himself. He cannot lift his head or hold a toy. He is, in the most literal sense of the word, utterly helpless.

Yet he touches so many people in such special ways.

He has touched me in a way that I cannot express.

He has been through more physical pain in his brief childhood than most people go through in a lifetime. Jacob may lack eyesight, yet he has shown so many people how to see life the way it is meant to be seen. He cannot speak, yet he communicates so many valuable lessons to so many people despite all of his disabilities. He loves life more than any one I have ever met. He shows me how to live each day to the fullest.

Jacob has taught me to take a situation, any situation, and make it positive. He has taught me to see life so differently, accept it for what it is, and accept people for who they are.

Jacob hasn't just inspired me and my family, he has inspired thousands. Because of Jacob we started Jacob's Ladder (the Canadian Foundation for the Control of Neurodegenerative Disease). It has become a million-dollar foundation funding research into neurodegenerative diseases, encouraging genetic screening for parents and parents-to-be, as well as sponsoring international prizes in the area of genetics. Jacob's Ladder has made huge strides in research, awareness, and education in the medical field.

Miracles do happen.

Jacob is a tribute to the wonder and joy of life, and continues to be the shining light in our life. He is eight as I write this book.

Jeff and Ellen pregnant with Jacob at forty weeks.

Chapter 1

I LOVED BEING PREGNANT.

I loved every kick, every pain, and every craving. I loved every pound I gained—all fifty-one of them! I loved that I didn't have to wear a coat in the winter. I loved that when there were huge lines to go to the bathroom I was led to the front. I loved that I had a massive tummy that I would rub all day and night.

I loved when other people rubbed my tummy.

I was scheduled to be induced on May 15, 1997. I remember driving down to the hospital with Jeff after a celebratory dinner with my family at one of my favourite restaurants. I felt more than ready for my new life. By then I had read all the books to help me prepare for childbirth. We had taken pre-natal classes. I had practised my Kegel exercises with practically religious devotion.

I was ready!

The nurses prepared me for labour by trying to soften my cervix with an ointment that was as uncomfortable as anything I had ever experienced. I thought that maybe this was good pain, like they talked about in all of those books. But my cervix wasn't softening at all.

The next step was to break my water and then put me on a drip to bring on contractions. Twenty-four hours later our first baby finally was ready to be pushed into the world.

It turned out to be not the easiest delivery—and didn't resemble any of the happy scenarios I had read so much about. My cervix was torn into four pieces and I needed more than one hundred internal stitches.

At one point, the doctor looked at me and said, "That's the last child you'll ever have."

I was hazy from the pain and fatigue of the procedure. But it was a brutal slap to the face. It was the first sign that my dream of motherhood might take some unexpected detours.

I looked at Jeff in complete disbelief and shock. "What does he mean this is the last child we will ever have?"

BECAUSE OF THE HEALTHY AMNIOCENTESIS TEST, I knew my baby was a boy.

I carried him for forty-one weeks. He had been one week overdue. So after all that time I was more than anxious to meet my little baby. After hours of pain, nothing else matters when you hear that you have a perfectly healthy nine-pound-one-ounce little boy. When the nurse handed him to me for the first time I felt something I had never felt before: an overwhelming surge of love. He was warm, and cuddly.

He was ours.

Mine.

He was perfect. He was beautiful.

I cuddled Jacob. I felt like sobbing with joy. I remember what that doctor had said to me. I put my face close to Jacob's and whispered, "Who cares if you are my last child? You will be my first child today and forever."

My family was waiting to meet the newest family member: beautiful, healthy, Jacob William Schwartz. This little baby was the first grandchild on my side of the family.

They were as proud and as happy as we were. I glowed.

When I first tried to nurse Jacob, however, something didn't seem right. Jacob wasn't eating properly. The two of us just couldn't seem to get a proper latch when I tried to nurse him. All of the books and pre-natal classes made nursing look so natural and easy. Every time Jacob would latch on, I would have to hold my breath and count to ten, because the pain was so excruciating.

I must be doing something wrong, I decided. I was determined to get it right. After many attempts and countless improvisations, I found I could just bear the pain, but the two of us took an incredibly long time to figure the whole feeding thing out.

As a first-time mom, I thought it was my fault, I just wasn't doing it right. I spoke to my friends, family, and three lactation consultants, and everyone had something different to say. There was nothing natural and easy about teaching each other how to nurse. I was so confused and frustrated. I didn't know whose advice to take.

Finally, I learned to follow Jacob's lead. For him it seemed like a game of bobbing for apples. Jacob loved it. He grew into what Jeff and I assumed proudly was a happy, chubby baby.

On the other hand, he cried all the time.

Jacob screamed day and night.

We figured it must be colic. Our family members would take turns coming over to take Jacob for walks, because somehow fresh air seemed to be the only way to stop him from crying.

I remember thinking how glad I was Jacob had been born in May, because if he was born in the winter I don't know what we would have done to stop him from crying. Thank goodness for the family because if they didn't help pitch in, I don't know how I would have gotten through those first few months.

Most children are colicky or finicky. For Jacob, however, his colic phase seemed increasingly a permanent feature. My maternal antenna was up and I realized that Jacob seemed nowhere close to the developmental milestones the books and experts had predicted.

Jeff and I had read every book about babies we could get our hands on. Were we overreacting? Should we just relax and let nature take its course?

A huge part of me was in denial about potential problems. I just did not want to face it. Jeff and I talked. We consulted.

Something was wrong with Jacob.

Jacob's eyes weren't tracking. If I dangled a toy in front of him and moved it from side to side his eyes would wander in an unfocused manner.

"Jakey," I would prompt sweetly. "Jakey, honey?" Again and again I would try to attract his attention, but it was like he was living within some completely self-contained world of his own.

Jacob had a large head that was not properly proportionate to the rest of his body. At a point where most infants begin lifting their heads on their own, Jacob's head would flop from one side to the other. Every time he lifted his head, it just came flopping down.

Something was wrong.

At Jacob's second-month checkup, his pediatrician decided that, indeed, he should have displayed more development by that time and that it would be prudent to have Jacob tested.

It was not easy hearing that our doctor agreed there was a problem, but I was encouraged, because I fully trusted Jacob's pediatrician. The specialists would quickly diagnose the problem, Jacob would be cured, and we three would resume the dream of our perfect life together as a happy family.

For two months, doctors at Toronto's Hospital for Sick Children conducted test after test in an attempt to pin down a diagnosis. When called upon to secure a sample of his blood, the nurses joked about the difficulty of finding a vein in his chubby little wrists and ankles.

But each day seemed to require yet another test.

There were CAT scans, and ultrasounds and MRIs and EEGs. It was an endless alphabet soup of tests.

Typically, Jacob would be laid out on the table like a helpless pin cushion as again and again he was prodded and poked with needles. For each test Jacob would have to lay perfectly still and quiet. As an inducement to relaxation—it was easiest if Jacob slept through the tests—we had to force him to drink chloral hydrate, a sedative. It is so bitter it makes you gag when you try to swallow it.

How do I know? I tried it myself before I gave it to Jacob the first time. What I had sampled was a tiny taste. Jeff and I had to lay him down and force him to drink five millilitres of this disgusting concoction.

Jacob would struggle. He would cry and scream. He would turn away and squirm. I would be forced to hold him down.

Between the endless stabbing pain of the needles, the forced restraint, the sedatives, and every other painful procedure, I felt like we were torturing him.

I hated to do it. I just wanted to scream, "Enough already!" But I knew that all of these tests were necessary, so I kept my screaming insides silent.

Jeff, Jacob, and I cried all through the tests. Each time Jacob wept himself to sleep as finally the sedation took effect. Then he was momentarily at peace. But there was nothing that Jeff and I could take to calm our nerves. The only thing that we had now was silence.

Another test required a biopsy of skin. Without sedation. The doctor scraped off what he had assured us would be a "small" section of skin from Jacob's right arm. Not surprisingly, Jacob howled. To my horror, the "small" section of skin impressed me as not so small at all. In fact, given how small his little arm was, the patch seemed huge.

Even at two months of age, however, Jacob was showing us that he was a fighter. Jacob would scream. And I mean scream. The kind of outraged screams that could peel paint off a wall at one hundred yards.

But my heart ached for him.

After all these painful tests, Jacob was terrified each and every time anyone tried to touch him. Even when I opened his diaper to change him his face would suddenly twist into an expression of helplessness and fear, as if to say, "What are you going to do to me now?!"

Despite all of the tests, after two months the doctors seemed no closer to a diagnosis.

Then one morning we got a call from the hospital's division of clinical and metabolic genetics at the Hospital for Sick Children. They wanted Jeff and me to come down to the hospital. They told us to leave Jacob at home.

We knew this couldn't be good news because they didn't need Jacob for any more tests. We thought, at least we could get some answers.

I kissed Jacob goodbye and told him that whatever it was, we could handle it. I told him that I would take care of him, and I would make sure that he would have a wonderful life.

I hugged him to give me the strength.

THE DRIVE DOWN WAS ONE OF THE LONGEST AND MOST excruciating drives of my life. We tried to guess what they would say. We had absolutely no clue what we were in for that day.

We talked about eventualities. We tried to prop each other up. We made pointless small talk.

A low drumbeat of dread began to sound in the back of my mind. I tried to banish the negativity. I thought hopeful thoughts.

I prayed.

At the hospital, the nurse who worked at the metabolic genetics clinic took us to a private room. We sat in this room for only a few minutes, but it seemed like hours. Ironically, I remember thinking what a relief it was to be in the room without Jacob.

No one was going to hurt him today.

The bright and cheery yellow walls of the room couldn't mask the black moment that I sensed was about to occur. The door swung open and the metabolic geneticist came in. She greeted us with a sympathetic smile and in a lovely South African accent introduced us to the medical student who accompanied her.

I thought, "How could anyone with such a beautiful accent tell us anything unpleasant?"

She sat down and gave us the news.

I was wrong. I was so wrong.

I heard the phrase "Canavan disease."

It sounded harmless. It sounded professional and remote. It had nothing to do with me. Nothing to do with Jacob.

"Jacob is going to suffer."

"No," I whimpered. "This cannot be happening."

"Most likely Jacob will die. The survival rate is poor."

"How poor?"

She shrugged and was silent.

I looked at Jeff. I wanted him to tell me that all of this wasn't true. I wanted him to stand up and tell these doctors that Jacob was going to be just fine. The two of us locked eyes and we couldn't say or do anything. We were completely helpless.

Why was this happening? Why Jacob? Why us?

After the geneticist and her student left the room, Jeff and I sat there. We were frozen. We didn't know what to do, or where to go. There was nothing we could say to each other. We just sat there together, in the silence.

We felt defeated.

Every time I tried to say something, I remained quiet. Jeff did the same thing. We left the hospital and drove to the beltline, a tree-lined path in the heart of Toronto. We attempted to make some kind of sense out of all of this. We walked down that path arm in arm, holding each other up.

When we got home, I ran into the house and hugged

Jacob tightly, like I never wanted to let go. Jacob's shirt was soaked with my tears.

He giggled.

I looked into his face—into his sightless eyes. Eyes that nevertheless seemed to twinkle with mirth.

He was smiling. I was sobbing—feeling as low and full of self-pity as I have ever experienced in my life—and he was grinning from ear to ear as if my sobbing was the most hilarious joke in the world.

Everything was going to be okay, his smile said.

❀ ❀ ❀

I CALLED MY PARENTS. I TRIED TO BE BRAVE, BUT I BROKE out into uncontrollable sobs when I heard my mother say hello.

My parents always do that to me. I can't seem to hide my true feelings because whenever I hear their voices I just let it all out. This time I knew that a Band-Aid wouldn't fix anything.

"Ellen, what's the matter? What's wrong?"

Jacob is my parents' first grandson. They waited anxiously for nine months to meet their first grandchild. My parents had such plans. They couldn't believe that their baby was having her own baby. Their joy was knowing that they didn't have to discipline their grandson.

This time around their big job was to spoil this child with love.

"Ellie?"

Jeff took the phone. He asked if they could come to our house. He asked them to call my brothers as well. Then Jeff called his sisters and his brother. This was going to be so hard. We could only manage to explain what the doctors had told us once.

That evening our families sat around our tiny living room. Everyone knew that we had news to share, but no one could have imagined the severity of it.

All I remember from that evening is sitting between my parents and squeezing their hands as Jeff—as calmly as he could manage—explained the diagnosis and Jacob's prognosis for the future.

I couldn't look at anyone's face.

All of our dreams had been completely shattered.

My parents sat there holding my hands, squeezing back. The comfort was incredible. I knew that they shared my pain, and it wasn't just my dream that had become a nightmare. I always knew that no matter what, I always had my family. This was the day that I needed them most and they were all there.

The next day my parents asked if they could take me out. They sensed that I needed to get outside and away for a few hours.

I didn't care where we were going, I was just happy to go somewhere. The three of us drove to a golf course. It was the perfect place for me to be. My mom and I rode in one cart and my father was in another. It was October and the leaves had changed but still clung to the branches. The fall colours were magnificent—red, yellow, green, brown, and orange.

I squeezed my mother's hand again and the two of us started to cry. We were thinking the same thing: Jacob would never be able to see this beautiful day. He would never be able to golf with his papa.

He would never get to do any of the things that any grandkid gets to do with his grandparents—silly everyday things we all take for granted.

We cried until the tears dried out.

Then we started to giggle. After three beautiful practice swings, my father muffed his shot right into the river.

PEOPLE ASK ME WHERE I GET MY STRENGTH FROM AND how I learned to be resilient. It's funny, because I do not think of myself as either emotionally strong or particularly resilient. The truth is, you become strong because there is no other choice. I was raised to accept whatever I have been handed and learn how to cope with it the best way possible. Life throws something at you and you either respond to it or you don't.

That silly muffed shot meant more to me than just a golf game. I realized that life was going to go on whether I liked it or not. Okay. Fact: Jacob will never be able to play golf. He won't be able to admire the scenery out the car window on family drives.

But he appreciates a good laugh. Just like his grandparents.

AFTER JACOB'S DIAGNOSIS, I HEARD FROM PEOPLE with whom I hadn't been in contact since grade school. The kindness and comfort that they shared in their letters and gifts from the heart raised my spirits.

One woman came over with this massive binder filled with everything ever written about Canavan disease. She attached a letter saying that giving information was the only way she knew how to help. She had done all the hard work. All Jeff and I just had to do was rifle through the three-inch binder filled with information about something that we really didn't want to read, but knew we had to.

When I opened it, a trio of words flew at me like startled birds: deadly, fatal, blind.

I couldn't deal with it.

I wanted to slam the binder shut. I wanted to shut this out of my life. I wanted a son who would sit on the couch and eat Cheerios. I wanted to look out the window and watch Jeff throw a ball to our son, and for our son to throw it back.

I wanted to be able to hear my child say, "I love you, Mommy."

I wanted to teach our son how to walk, ride, swim, and play. Jacob would never be able to do any of those things.

These are the facts: Canavan disease is a rare, inherited, fatal neurodegenerative disorder for which there is no known treatment or cure. It is one of a group of disorders called leukodystrophies that cause imperfect growth or development of the myelin sheath, the fatty covering that acts as an insulator around nerve fibres in the brain. Myelin lends its colour to the white matter of the brain. Children with Canavan disease are unable to produce an enzyme called aspartoacylase, which is needed to produce myelin. Without myelin, the white matter of the brain degenerates into spongy tissue riddled with microscopic fluid-filled spaces. Nerve cells need myelin to function properly. Canavan disease causes progressive brain atrophy.

Canavan disease is named for Myrtelle Canavan, who first described the disorder in 1931. Infants with the disease appear normal at birth. When the child is around three to nine months parents notice subtle changes. One of the earliest signs of Canavan disease recognized by many parents is lack of head control. The child is found to be "floppy." We recognized that from our experience. Children with the disease cannot crawl, walk, sit, or talk. Over time they may suffer seizures, become paralyzed, or blind, and have trouble swallowing. Their hearing remains sharp and they continue to recognize and respond to the voices of their primary caregivers.

Canavan disease, like Tay-Sachs, is an inherited disorder. Although Canavan disease may occur in any ethnic group, it is most frequent among Ashkenazi Jews from eastern Poland, Lithuania, and western Russia. My grandparents came from that area and so did Jeff's. It is estimated that one in forty Ashkenazi Jews is a carrier of the Canavan gene. Both parents must be carriers of the defective gene in order to have an affected child. If neither, or only one, parent carries a mutation, the couple is not at risk for having a child with Canavan disease. If both parents are carriers, there is a one in four chance with each pregnancy that their child will have Canavan disease. Jeff and I both carry this defective gene. Without knowing it, we passed it to our son.

The prognosis for victims of Canavan disease is poor. Death usually occurs before age four, although some children may survive into their teens and twenties.

There is no cure. There is no therapy or treatment.

Except support and love.

I HAD HOPED THAT GRAPPLING WITH THE FACTS MIGHT allow me to deal more constructively with my grief. That knowledge might replace doubt and uncertainty and that would help me over the hump. But it only made me feel more lonely, scared, and depressed. None of my friends or family members had ever experienced anything like this. I was convinced no one could understand my feelings.

For weeks on end I walked around with my heart at street level. I couldn't raise my spirits. I couldn't talk to Jeff. I couldn't talk to anyone. I just wanted to hold Jacob and cry.

I was so angry. I felt so ripped off.

I couldn't believe that God would allow this to happen to me. I tried to pray, but I couldn't. I stopped believing in God. I thought that no God could ever do anything like this, to a child... to my child.

Everywhere I looked mothers were with their children. Their children were walking, talking, and looking at them.

My Jacob would never walk with me, or talk to me or look at me.

One day I was sitting in a Starbucks. Jacob was in his stroller at my side, sleeping. I was indulging myself, having a coffee and enjoying the newspaper.

Three women at the table beside me were talking.

"I can't believe it. My son tried out for the select team and didn't make it. We are so disappointed."

"Oh no," her companion commiserated. "That's just awful."

I was so angry. I wanted to yell at them. "How can you be concerned about your son making it onto the team, when my son may not make it to three!"

Weeks later in the same situation, I actually said something.

Two mothers were standing in line behind me waiting for our coffees. They were huddled in a discussion about the unsatisfactory grades on their children's report cards. I couldn't believe that these mothers were so worked up about grades.

I turned and addressed them both. "Just be grateful for what you have."

I hated myself because I felt so bitter and so angry. I felt that the world should pay for what happened. I didn't want to even shop for clothing for Jacob. I thought it was such a waste of time—he was just going to die. I actually walked into a shop to buy a snowsuit for Jacob and expected a reduced price because he would never wear it out. I was so upset that the owner wouldn't sell me the snowsuit at a discount that I stomped out in tears because I thought that no one could understand me.

In my wallowing self-pity I even wondered if I was being punished for an experience that had occurred a few months earlier. Jeff and I had been asked to play wheelchair hockey with a group of severely disabled children at Bloorview Macmillan, a home for children with disabilities. I had never been around anyone who had serious disabilities.

We walked into the gym and saw these helpless little children in wheelchairs. This was a whole new world and culture for me. I tried to mask my discomfort—my fear—but I had no idea how to talk to children who couldn't answer me.

One little boy took a liking to me and he kept smiling at me. His eyes said so much but his body wouldn't let him do anything but groan. He became my partner that day and I ran around the gym with him. I became his legs and arms.

A smile never left his face. Tears never left mine.

Walking back to the car after that event I told Jeff that I never wanted to do that again. I hated seeing those children. I couldn't stand watching them suffer. I felt that life was so cruel. Why would God allow children to be so sick? When I read about Canavan and thought about what Jacob would be, I remembered those children in the gym. I couldn't believe I was having one of those children.

I was convinced I could never deal with it.

Chapter 2

MOST PEOPLE GET TO CELEBRATE THEIR BIRTHDAYS once a year.

Every day is a birthday for Jacob. Each day we thank our lucky stars that he is still with us for another day.

May 17, Jacob's birthday, is a milestone in our house.

I remember.

We are all at the family cottage. It is a warm, sunny weekend, the first weekend after a long, cold winter. Everyone is invited up to celebrate. This is indeed a celebration. Our adorable, wide-eyed, chubby-cheeked, happy little boy is turning one.

Jacob seems happy. He is smiling and laughing.

I remember the dry and maddeningly calm and unemotional words of the prognosis: "Death usually occurs before age three or four."

MOST CHILDREN ARE TAKING THEIR FIRST STEPS AT that age and saying their first words. We were trying to teach Jacob to raise his head.

I would lie on my back with Jacob lying on my tummy. I would press his elbows against my chest to prop up the upper part of his back and I would say over and over again, "Up, up, up, up. Come on Jakey, you can do it! Up, up, up!" He would raise his head ever so slowly with determination and effort. Once his head was up, he would smile with accomplishment. Everyone in the room would cheer him on. Jacob had lifted his head.

That first birthday party was wonderful. We dressed the little prince in a bright yellow T-shirt and funky shorts and sat him in his reclining high chair. We turned the lights out and started to sing "Happy Birthday" to Jacob for the first time. As I walked in carrying the blue and white birthday cake, everyone was singing as loudly as they could.

Jacob's lower lip suddenly began to quiver and he burst out crying. Our happiness had scared him. We took it down a notch. The happy smile returned. The day was incredible. Our little boy was one.

I understood deep down that the only way I was ever going to accept the situation was to embrace Jacob's diagnosis as fully as possible. I could not afford to delude myself or have false hopes. But I just couldn't get past the fact that he was going to leave me some day. And more than likely—a some day that could come very soon.

Next year, for instance. Or next month.

Or tomorrow.

I had to understand death. I had to force myself to open my mind to spiritual thinking or I would never be able to live my life, or to accept Jacob's fate. I tried reading book after book. Nothing grabbed me until I opened *Many Masters, Many Lives* by Brian L. Weiss, former head of the psychiatry department at Mount Sinai Medical Center in Miami Beach.

The book gave me exactly what I needed. I needed to believe that there was life after death. I needed to know that Jacob wasn't put on this earth to suffer and die young. I needed to know that Jacob's life had a purpose. I needed to understand why Jacob was here for his sake.

I was beginning to understand.

Maybe Jacob was here for the rest of the world.

I know that sounds highfalutin. Weiss's book had awakened my spiritual side so much, however, that I had to learn more. I spoke to many prominent rabbis about death. They all confirmed that we are here to learn lesson in life and once those lessons are learned we can move on to a better place, a better world.

But what did that have to do with Jacob? What could have been the reason that he was born as he was? I felt that I was coming to terms with the deeper lessons he was teaching me. But a question kept spinning around in my head.

What was Jacob getting out of this?

Some religious people look at Jacob and feel God's presence. Some religious people even stand up when Jacob comes into the room because they feel he is on a higher spiritual level.

I believe it. I think that Jacob has learned the lessons we all desperately need to learn. He isn't able to make mistakes and he isn't able to learn from them because he doesn't need to. He doesn't need to feel guilt because it is not necessary for him. I believe that Jacob is here because he was missing one thing—that one thing being love.

Why else would someone be born without the ability do anything but look beautiful, smile, and cry? He is so easy to love and he is loved by so many. Jacob spends most of his days cuddled in people's arms. Jacob isn't able to ask for love but he receives it with more gratification than any other person.

I know that once Jacob has received the love that he so desperately needs he will move on to a better place. I'm not sure where that place is, but I know that it will be somewhere special, somewhere we will all hope to go. All you have to do is look into his deep brown eyes and you see the lively spirit trapped inside his helpless body. Once Jacob is ready, that trapped spirit will fly.

THE YEAR JACOB TURNED ONE, WE WERE TOLD ABOUT groundbreaking, experimental gene replacement therapy going on at Yale University in New Haven, Connecticut. Scientists would inject a synthetic gene into the brains of Canavan patients with the hope of producing myelin. The trial would be taking place in September. Since Jacob would only be sixteen months of age and many of his nerve cells wouldn't have died yet, he was a prime candidate for this procedure.

But all the surgeries involved were totally invasive and we had no way of preparing Jacob for what could happen. After all the pain he had been forced to suffer already, the idea of subjecting him to even more—and for iffy results? It seemed....

We were torn.

We consulted all Jacob's doctors: his pediatrician, his genetic metabolic doctors, his neurologist, and his neurosurgeon. We spoke to our family, friends, and to other families with Canavan children.

The trial would be painful for Jacob. But that was just one phase of the risk. First, neurosurgeons at the Hospital for Sick Children would have to insert a shunt into Jacob's brain to receive the synthetic gene. We would then fly to New Haven to stay at Yale for the two-week procedure and recovery. Then we would have to follow up with an MRI four times a year at the Children's Hospital of Philadelphia.

This was a lot of pain and suffering for something that might not even work. Not to mention the financial costs: the air fares, the hospital fees, the hotels. We didn't want Jacob to be a guinea pig, but we didn't have a choice. If the therapy didn't work, at least we would know that we did everything possible to try to make Jacob better. Jeff and I agreed that this was Jacob's only hope and our only chance to live a normal life.

We enrolled Jacob in the program.

In September 1998, Jacob's surgery in Toronto went without a hitch. He was such a trooper. After his surgery, he was recuperating in the recovery room. I lay down beside him. I whispered in his ear "Jakey, Jakey, Jakey." He just moved his lips to smile a weak smile. After all the tests, all of the pokes, all of the painful surprises, Jacob still trusted me.

But I felt that I had let him down. I was his mother, and I was supposed to protect him from harm. I allowed all of these doctors to hurt him. I hated the fact that this was only the beginning. It was only going to get worse, and we were gambling that these procedures would actually help Jacob. How could I allow other people to hurt my son, without his knowledge or consent?

But I just knew that if we didn't go through with this trial, I would always be wondering what if? If the therapy didn't work, at least I would know that Jeff and I did everything humanly possible to try to make Jacob better.

Ten days after the shunt was inserted into Jakey's brain we packed our bags and flew to Philadelphia. We checked in at Children's Hospital of Philadelphia for a baseline MRI before boarding a train to Yale University. The flight to Philadelphia foreshadowed the events that would follow the gene replacement therapy.

It was the most terrifying flight I'd ever experienced. The pilot was trying to land in Philadelphia through a furious thunderstorm. But whenever we descended through the clouds there was severe turbulence. Just as we were about to land, up we went again. The pilot aborted the landing three times. Jacob was on my lap and I was thinking that this was it for all of us. And Jacob? He loved the ride. He was giggling and laughing the whole way down.

We finally arrived in New Haven and checked into the hospital for our stay. Jeff and I met other families with children. There were sixteen children in the study, each one with the same disorder as our Jakey. During our visit, we met four other families. All the children were adorable and sick, and all the parents were loving, and totally devoted to their children. They all cuddled and hugged their children with the same love, warmth, and concern Jeff and I did with Jacob. We were all completely devastated, and hopeful that this therapy might help our children. I looked at the other children, and thought to myself, these poor parents. Yet I didn't think feel that way about Jeff and me. Somehow we were all in the same boat, yet I felt like we were on different oceans.

The other parents were completely focused on finding the cure for Canavan disease. They believed completely in this experimental therapy. Jeff and I valued their dedication and determination, but felt pessimistic about a cure. We knew that this was a long shot and that the probability for a cure was extremely unlikely. We were giving this therapy only one chance.

THE SIGHT OF ALL THE SICK LITTLE BABIES WHO OCCUPIED the rooms on the floor was devastating. I wanted to make everyone feel better, including myself. I cruise from room to room, pushing Jacob in his stroller, trying to find a mother

I could relate to—someone who would smile at me, someone to connect with.

Bonnie was one mother that I related to and we talked. I told her about Jacob and she told me all about her situation. Her son was experiencing recurring grand mal seizures, seizures that would last for extremely long periods of time.

As we were leaving the hospital, Bonnie came to say goodbye and gave me a bag from Victoria's Secret. "Ellen," she said, "I wanted you to have something."

I couldn't understand why someone who was practically a stranger wanted to give me a present. "Everyday you walk by our room and give me the most beautiful smile. I look forward to seeing you every day because somehow that smile tells me that everything is going to be okay. I just thought that if this mother could smile, then I can smile as well. This is my way to thank you for helping me through this, for giving me the strength to carry on."

The present was a pair of the softest pyjamas I had ever felt. "If you can't feel safe," she said, "then you might as well be comfortable." Seven years later, I still wear those pyjamas every night.

The pain and suffering Jacob endured during the recovery period after the gene replacement therapy was unimaginable. His head was wrapped in so many bandages he looked like a Smurf. Either Jeff or I would lay down on the hospital bed and Jacob would lay on top of us. This was his only comfortable position. Sometimes we would stay in this position for hours at a time, afraid to move even a finger or a toe, in fear that Jacob would wake up. We felt completely helpless as parents, and so far away from home.

We left Yale five days after Jacob's surgery to return to Toronto. We checked into a hotel for one night before taking the journey home. We wanted to be certain Jacob would remain stable enough for the trip.

We laid Jacob on the bed and undressed him. We opened his diaper to change him and suddenly he started to squeal with delight. It was as if he knew that he wasn't in a hospital anymore. We watched Jacob celebrate his freedom.

Day by day, little by little, Jacob regained his strength. And one month later Jacob had fully recovered from the gene replacement therapy. Life started to become relatively normal, and we enjoyed watching Jacob smile, giggle, and laugh.

I enrolled Jacob in a baby music class because he seemed to have a magical connection with music. All the other eighteen-month-olds would clap their hands, dance to the beat, and march around. Jacob could only lie in my lap, but his eyes would dance to the music. Every week Jacob and I would join twelve other mothers with their healthy children around the circle and listen to the wonderful sounds Kayla, the instructor, could make with her voice. Kayla makes different kinds of noises and sounds with her mouth. She can sound like a trumpet, a cello, or an oboe. He heard her voice and his eyes lit up and he tried to sing along and he was laughing. Kayla saw this little boy and she fell in love with him and he fell in love with her.

Jacob was stable and happy. Finally, we were in a routine.

❀ ❀ ❀

THAT OCTOBER, JEFF AND I WERE INVITED TO A wedding in Chicago.

An extremely close, childhood friend was getting married and I really wanted to go. My parents were going as well. Jeff and I weren't ready to leave Jacob with a sitter overnight so Jeff decided to stay home. I was excited to stay in a hotel room, catch up on some sleep, dress up, go to a wonderful party, and tour the city with my parents. I knew that Jeff and Jacob would love the one-on-one time together. And, to tell you the truth, I was ready for a break.

Off we went. I had a latte on the plane. I read *People* magazine cover-to-cover. There was no guilt. I knew that Jacob was with his daddy. I could totally enjoy myself. And I did, for most of the trip.

The wedding was beautiful. Late that evening, my parents walked me to my hotel room door and kissed me goodnight. I told them that I had the greatest trip and that this was exactly what I had needed. We said, "I love you," and went to bed.

Just as I was drifting off into a peaceful sleep there was a knock at the door. It was 2:30 AM I squinted through the peephole and saw my parents. I opened the door.

"Jeff just called," my dad said. "He wanted to make sure that we were with you when you heard the news. Jacob is in the hospital. He had a two-hour seizure, and the doctors don't know if he will ever wake up."

Just then the telephone rang. It was Jeff calling from the intensive care unit. Jacob had started to cry uncontrollably at 9 PM and wouldn't stop. He started to throw up and his temperature rose to over 104 degrees. His eyes had rolled back in his head and his whole body started to shake. Jeff couldn't stop the tremors. He called an ambulance and they rushed them to Sick Kids Hospital.

We couldn't get a flight until 6:30 AM I was trapped in Chicago as our nineteen-month-old baby was fighting for his life. I didn't know if I would ever see my little boy again. For three hours my mother and I lay together in spoon position and cried. She kept brushing her fingers through my hair telling me that everything was going to be all right. We both knew that her words did not ring true, but there was nothing else to say.

We finally arrived in Toronto. I have absolutely no idea how we travelled from the airport to the hospital I just remember running down the long corridor to the ICU. I desperately needed to see my baby boy and my husband. Jacob was lying on the hospital bed with tubes attached everywhere. He was hooked up to every monitor possible. He was pale and his face was so swollen that he was hardly recognizable.

FROM OCTOBER 10, 1998, TO DECEMBER 25, WE LIVED at the hospital.

As it turns out, Jacob had experienced severe complications from the gene-replacement therapy one month earlier. He was diagnosed with meningitis, an infection in the brain. Due to the meningitis, he also developed hydrocephalus, an increased amount of fluid in the brain that caused swelling.

The doctors doubted he would survive.

He was injected with incredibly strong antibiotics to combat the meningitis. Controlling the hydrocephalus demanded a much more invasive procedure. When he was stronger, a special shunt would be surgically placed into Jacob's brain to drain and regulate the fluid retention.

After five long days and nights living in the ICU, Jacob seemed to gather enough strength to give us a little smile. We would sing to him, or call his name repeatedly. He would open and then close his eyes. We knew that he knew who we were, and that gave us the strength to do whatever we had to in order to hopefully take Jacob home with us again.

Every day Jeff and I watched Jacob slowly get stronger. His skin colour went from a pale blue to pink. He started to breathe on his own without assistance. Eventually the doctors took away his oxygen. They started to take out each tube one by one. They unhooked the heart monitors. Finally, the only tube that stayed was his feeding tube, which ran up through his nose and down to his stomach. Jacob was dependant on this for nutrition, as his little body was too weak to eat any thing by mouth. Finally, we could pick Jacob up, and hold him in our arms free from the clutter of tubes, connections, and machines.

Jeff and I alternated nights at the hospital and I took a leave of absence from my teaching job. The meningitis had subsided and Jacob was ready to go into surgery to control the hydrocephalus. Somehow the fluid in his brain had to be drained. Neurosurgeons needed to insert a ventriculoperitoneal shunt into his brain. This shunt would transfer the fluid from the brain into the abdominal cavity. Complications occurred after each operation. Jacob would go into surgery only to come out with his head wrapped in a turban of bandages and every time he seemed to begin to recover he would experience leakage, or infection. In four months, Jacob had seven brain operations. He was terrified of everyone and everything around him. Whenever we would try to change his diaper he would scream out with fear because he didn't want any more pain.

Jeff and I established a rule with the hospital staff. Whenever Jacob was in our arms or in his bed no one was allowed to touch him. He needed a safe place. If a procedure had to be done, they would take him to the procedure room. He needed to know that there were places where he wouldn't be hurt. Jacob couldn't see the needle coming. He couldn't anticipate what was going to happen to him. Jeff and I had to make sure that he felt safe.

After the third attempt to administer a shunt, we decided that we couldn't allow Jacob to go through this agony anymore. We couldn't watch Jacob continually fight knowing that his disease was progressive and this was only a temporary solution that was not even working. Enough was enough. He wasn't going to experience any more pain if we could help it. We began to discuss palliative care because Jacob's quality of life had deteriorated and we weren't sure if he would recover.

Kayla wanted to know why her new little friend wasn't coming to the classes. When she heard that her little buddy was living down at the hospital, she sent Jacob his own personal Kayla CD.

I was touched that she actually thought about Jacob and cared enough to send him a recording. I called her to thank her for her kind gesture. She asked if she could come and sing to him. Jacob was in between surgeries at the time and we couldn't get a response from him. We were in a terrible place emotionally.

Kayla came with her guitar in and her partner Queenie. As the two of them sat by Jacob's bedside, Kayla started playing her guitar, and Jacob started to smile. She didn't just make Jacob smile that day, she brought Jacob back to us.

The chief of neurosurgery at the hospital said, "Let's try one more time." One more time! That was it.

So Jacob was prepped for surgery again. The team of doctors and nurses were taking our little boy away to the operating room for the fourth time. I lay with Jacob on the hospital bed until I was forced to leave him. Jeff spoke to the anaesthesiologist, answering questions that he had answered so many times before. We couldn't help but wonder why they just didn't read the ten-inch chart that sat on the foot of the bed. Instead we did what we were supposed to, and Jeff just answered all of the questions pertaining to Jacob's health. We waited until the surgery room was prepped. A nurse and a hospital porter came through the two automatic doors labelled "Hospital Personnel Only" and told us that it was time. I kissed Jacob and squeezed him tightly, then rose up off of the bed, leaving Jacob alone. Jeff and I stood there, holding each other, as they rolled Jacob away for the fourth time. We felt like our hearts were being ripped right out of our bodies. We had no choice but to helplessly sit and wait.

The neurosurgeon finally came out and led us into the private waiting room attached to the surgical waiting room where the surgeons informed parents about the results of their child's operation. He told us that he thought that the surgery went well and we would have to wait and see how Jacob recovers. He told us that he couldn't believe the inner strength that Jacob had and that he thought that Jacob would pull through.

Jacob did pull through and recovered beautifully. He slowly began to smile, then giggle, then laugh. We were finally able to pull off all the bandages and Jacob started to look like Jacob again. We knew that we were on borrowed time but we didn't care. We were so thrilled to have our boy back. I couldn't wait to lie on my bed, with Jeff at my side, and Jacob lying between us. We would tickle him, kiss him, squeeze him, and watch him laugh and enjoy his little life.

After he got out of the hospital, after all of the surgeries, after the gene therapy and everything that went with it, we decided he'd cried more than he ever needed to in a lifetime. All Jacob wants from life is to be loved. All we want from Jacob is for him to be happy and never to feel pain again.

Chapter 3

BY THE TIME MAY ROLLED AROUND, WE WERE READY to celebrate Jacob's second birthday. We were proud that our Jacob had endured all that and we wanted to show our tough, resilient little treasure off to everyone.

Jacob's second birthday was another huge milestone. Most two-year-olds can walk, run, eat, speak, play, and joke around. Most parents are afraid to take their eyes off their terrible twos because of their energy and the mischief they can get into.

We were afraid to take our eyes off Jacob, fearing that might not wake up. He had survived a two-and-a-half hour seizure, a drug-induced coma, hydrocephalus, meningitis, discussions of palliative care, discussions of inserting a gastric tube (or g-tube), and seven operations to his brain.

Doctors expected him to die.

Jacob had other plans. Like celebrating his second birthday.

JEFF AND I INVITED THIRTY-SEVEN TWO- AND THREE-year-olds to our backyard. We rented a massive jumping castle for the occasion and brought in bunches and bunches of helium balloons. We chose the theme of the Toronto Maple Leafs hockey team, because Jacob loved to cuddle with Jeff and cheer on the Leafs. Every time Jeff would yell, "He scores," Jacob would laugh out loud.

We had spent hours planning when we should have been watching the weather forecast. Our celebratory picnic outside was going to be a wash-out and we had to move Jacob's party inside fast.

All the parents and children sat in a circle and Kayla led the room in a special singsong for Jacob. He loved every minute of it. I loved the fact that everything seemed so normal. Jacob didn't give up living, and we wouldn't either. We wanted everyone to celebrate Jacob's life, and not feel sorry for him or us.

Jacob was feeling better. His new baby sister was on the way. Family and friends surrounded us and everyone was so happy. The future seemed bright.

Inevitably, the idea of more childred surfaced.

Jeff and I wanted to have a family, but after Jacob we were terrified. We knew there was a one in four chance that our next baby would be affected with Canavan disease. We cherished Jacob but we couldn't even imagine putting another child through the same thing. We knew that we were going to lose our first-born and there was absolutely no way that we would go through that again.

It seemed selfish on our part to even consider it.

And yet...

Further complicating our plans was the bad news my doctor had "delivered" in the delivery room: "That's the last child you will ever have." I had been heartbroken. Jeff and I talked about it. Ultimately, we decided not to give up hope before fully investigating our options.

Jeff and I went to see a high-risk specialist at Women's College Hospital. We explained what our doctor had said. Should we just accept the fact that I could not have any more children?

It turns out we were wrong!

Our new obstetrician—in a surprisingly matter-of-fact manner—informed us that we most certainly could have more children and that all that was required would be an insertion of what was known as a "cervical cerclage stitch." This stitch would allow me to carry a baby to term. We desperately wanted another child and thanks to chronic villus sampling (cvs), a method of prenatal diagnosis for parents that have children at risk for genetic diseases that lets you determine whether the next baby will be affected by the beginning of the second trimester of pregnancy, we could.

Luckily I don't have difficulty getting pregnant but I panicked when I was pregnant with our second child. I walked around trying to pretend that I wasn't pregnant. I couldn't enjoy the incredible miracle of pregnancy because I felt like I had to protect myself. I worried about it day and night. Finally, on the day of my cvs, three months into my second pregnancy, I lay perfectly still while the doctors took a sample of the placenta for DNA analysis. The results would come in a minimum of ten days. Those ten days seemed like an eternity. All I did was worry.

We finally received the call. The baby was affected. It had Canavan disease. That news alone was unbelievably demoralizing, but imagine having to terminate the same pregnancy twice. I found out I was born with a bi-corneal uterus (a uterus divided in two). The day after I terminated the pregnancy Jeff and I had to go back to the hospital for a routine ultrasound, just to make sure that everything was fine after the procedure. Suddenly, the technician looked at me with utter shock. There was a heartbeat. The doctors had missed it. They had gone up the wrong side of my uterus. We had to do the procedure all over again.

A few months later we decided to get pregnant again, and I spent another three months ignoring my pregnancy. Jacob was stable and happy and I knew that whatever happened with this pregnancy was meant to be.

The CVS test came back negative for Canavan disease. My joy at the moment was unbounded. I was nearly breathless with happiness. We immediately made an appointment for a cerclage stitch procedure.

Nine months later, Beverly Danielle Schwartz was born. Another miracle is that Beverly isn't even a carrier of Canavan disease. Like hawks, Jeff and I watched Beverly develop.

Beverly was a dream child. She did everything that the books told us that she would do. We couldn't believe that she could actually lift her head with ease. She followed me with her eyes when I moved. She smiled at us when we smiled. She could nurse easily. She slept through the night at four months. She ate and drank without difficulty. She sat up at six months, just like the books said she should. She said "Mommy" and "Daddy." She had a sparkle and a twinkle in her eyes that lit up the room.

She helped us enjoy Jacob even more because we had normalcy in our home. We felt like everyone else now. We thought that with Beverly, we could do what other families do. We could teach her how to swim, how to throw a ball, how to ride a bike, and how to blow bubbles. We would be able to celebrate every single milestone that she achieved, and enjoy every moment with her.

WHEN JACOB IS HEALTHY, SOMETHING RESEMBLING A normal life is possible. But Jacob's health can change on a dime. One moment he seems fine, but in a snap his health can rapidly deteriorate. Because of Jacob's inability to move, the phlegm stays in one place and can't move around. He easily developed infections. He has difficulty controlling his secretions. His little body has difficulty fighting off sicknesses. When other children get a cough and a cold, Jacob gets pneumonia.

Every time a child comes into our house with a runny nose I am terrified. This includes my own children. We are constantly washing our hands and sneezing into our elbows.

At school I am surrounded by children and their germs, and I am careful not to bring anything home with me. Whenever I come home from teaching, I immediately run upstairs to change and wash up.

Jacob can't put his hand on his stomach or his head to tell me in words what hurts. With Jacob it is a guessing game. When he hurts, his body just shuts down. He becomes extremely weak, his eyes roll back and his lids flutter slowly. He turns whitish blue and his breathing sounds like a rattling drum. Every breath is shallow, laboured, and a struggle.

When these symptoms occur, and they often do, Jacob will go to sleep. We lay him on his side on his hospital bed. This seems to help him breathe better and his little lungs can battle the fluid in his lungs. We sit at his bedside holding on to the suction machine anxiously waiting for a cough. We have to help Jacob clear the fluid because his body is too weak to help itself. We have to continually hit his ribs hoping to loosen some of the phlegm.

Jacob sleeps.

Every four hours we give him Ventolin and Flovent to decrease the inflammation of his lungs and open the airway in order to help him breathe better. We insert the puffer into an air chamber that covers Jacob's mouth and nose. We push the puffer in and wait for Jacob to take in four breaths.

Jacob sleeps.

We turn him and change his diaper every two hours during the day and every four hours at night.

He sleeps.

We crush up Tylenol and insert it into a syringe with water. We give him baclofen, a muscle relaxant needed to help his stiffness and spasms. We give him nitrazepam to control any possible seizure activity. These meds are administered every four hours and inserted into his g-tube daily.

He sleeps.

We slow down Jacob's feeding rate so that his weak body can digest his food and drink. The key is to keep him hydrated. We attach the container holding his liquid meal to an intravenous pole beside his bed and slide the pump into its holder half way down the pole. We listen to the continuous whir of the pump pumping nutrition into Jacob. We do whatever possible to avoid hospitalization.

When Jacob is home, either sick or healthy, at least there is a sense of routine. When Jacob is admitted to hospital, life turns upside down. One of us lives at the hospital while the other takes care of Beverly (we would end up having a third child, which made our daily routines even more chaotic!) and the household duties. We are constantly running back and forth to the hospital. Jacob is constantly prodded and poked until something is found.

It doesn't seem fair that Jacob has to become so ill so often. He has suffered enough. He has shown his resilience and his desire to live. He shouldn't have to suffer colds and coughs like the rest of us. He should be exempt. He just can't seem to find a break.

Sometimes when he is sick, waiting for that beautiful smile seems like an eternity. I watch over his long, lean body and look at the great big mop of red hair. I marvel at his perfectly rounded lips and his adorable little nose. I stare at his closed eyelids and see his eyeballs roll from side to side and I can't help wondering what he could possibly be thinking about. His eyes are so active, but trapped inside a body that won't move. His eyelashes are so long they seem to tangle when closed together.

Sometimes when he is sleeping so peacefully, I can't help but wish that he wouldn't wake up because watching Jacob suffer is heartbreaking. I don't want him to feel any more pain. Sometimes I wish that he would wake up, open his eyes, look at me, see me, and say, "Hi, Mom." Sometimes I just watch him and tears roll down my face. He is so helpless. When he is sick, I am sick. When he is happy, I am better.

Chapter 4

YET ANOTHER MILESTONE.

With Jacob, we were learning more and more about what it means to be alive and to fight to survive.

At age three, we enrolled Jacob in an integrated nursery school five minutes from where we lived. Play and Learn is affiliated with Bloorview Macmillan Children's Centre, a world-renowned rehabilitation centre in Toronto for children with disabilities. Play and Learn is a special place: a safe environment where Jacob could be accepted for himself. The teachers want to bring out the best in every child who attend the school.

In Jacob's class were eight children with varying special needs and eight children who were perfectly healthy. The concept of the school is brilliant. The children learned from each other. The children with special needs have other children to imitate and follow, while the healthy children learn patience and empathy for others. The other little children would sit with Jacob and sing to him as if it was the most natural thing in the world.

The first teacher Jacob met picked him up, carried him into the room, and spoke to him in such a loving and understanding manner that for the first time Jeff and I didn't feel we had to say, "Be careful of his head" or "This is how you pick him up." They knew.

They actually expected me to go away for two hours. I couldn't believe that I was actually supposed to drop Jacob off for nursery school, just like all moms. They expected me to drop him off and carry on my morning without Jacob. Play and Learn taught me that Jacob could go to school. Play and Learn gave me a life.

Many mornings I stood outside the classroom, peering in. I would see the teachers lay Jacob in a large bin filled with uncooked lima beans and help manoeuvre his arms and legs around the bin so that he could feel the cool, smoothness of these beans between his fingers and toes. Jacob would cuddle on his teacher's lap during circle time and enjoy the wonderful animated stories and songs that were taught to all of the kids. They would take battery-operated toys hooked up to a large button so Jacob could play with them with as much pleasure as any kid in the room.

When everyone went outside to run, climb and play, Jacob would, too. His teachers pulled him around in the wagon, and the other children pulled him as well. The teachers sat in the sand with him, took off his socks and ran his feet through the sand. When the other children went to the washroom, Jacob had his diaper changed. He was part of the group, and the group loved him.

I would find him nestled in a teacher's lap enjoying music circle with Wayne. Wayne, the music teacher, is a free spirit with a long braided ponytail that reaches down to his lower back. The children gravitate to him as he walks around Play and Learn strumming his guitar and singing to the children with warmth and enthusiasm. When he started to play "The Lion Sleeps Tonight," he would introduce the song by saying, "Hey everyone, here's a song for my buddy Jacob." When Jacob would hear this introduction his feet would start to move and his mouth would open wide with excitement.

FOR HIS THIRD BIRTHDAY, WE INVITED JACOB'S whole class, parents, teachers, and Wayne to our house for lunch in the backyard. Unlike Jacob's second birthday, this May 17 was a magnificent spring day. The weather was perfect for a picnic.

We set up picnic tables in a row and put Jacob, the king, in his special chair at the head of the table. Beverly and Jacob's cousins sat on either side of him with his buddies from school all around. Jacob was part of the group. He had friends, and everyone thought he was special.

One mother presented us with a gift from the whole class. It looked like a large painting, but it was wrapped with brown paper covered with designs that all the children in his class had created. I lay the present in front of Jacob and held his hands so that he could open his own present.

It was a framed collage created by all of Jacob's friends at Play and Learn. This same mother orchestrated this exceptional gift. She had the teachers trace handprints of each of the children. The children painted and cut out their handprints and glued them onto a piece of Bristol board in the form of a circle. Each child glued his or her photo into the palm of their handprint. Jacob's print was in the middle of this circle of hands.

I looked at this gift and tears just rolled down my cheeks. I didn't know how to thank this exceptional group of people. I hoped that my tears and facial expressions showed the appreciation that a gift like this deserved. This was a gift given right from the heart. I looked around the table and all I saw was fifteen very special young children, with so many different needs and so many different abilities and disabilities. One thing for sure, they all knew how to celebrate, and what a celebration it was.

Play and Learn taught me that Jacob could go to school just like any other child. He could play and he could learn.

Jeff and I were having trouble playing and learning from each other. Jacob's prognosis put a lot of pressure on our marriage. Jeff and I often fought. We were two completely different people trying to cope with a shattered future in two completely different ways.

We were also completely sleep deprived. Because of his illness Jacob's only slept for a couple hours at a time. For two years Jeff and I would both be up between 2 AM and 5 AM looking out for Jacob. We were taking care of our children, working at our jobs, trying to have a relationship, and not sleeping. Something had to give, and inevitably our marriage suffered.

Let me give you a bit of history. As a child I had a life that most people dream about. I grew up in beautiful home, in a safe and gracious neighbourhood surrounded by loving people. I was the princess, born between two princes. I admired and idolized my two brothers and I still do. My brothers were sports fanatics, so I spent a lot of time playing basketball, ball hockey, football, baseball, and tennis. My parents loved to laugh. They adored each other and still do. My father worked extremely hard and played extremely hard. He would take each of us on special trips with him and there was nothing more valuable than that one-on-one time with Dad. My mom coddled us when we were sick, scolded us when we misbehaved, and made sure that our heads were screwed on right.

Meeting Jeff was an extension of the life that I was accustomed to living. He was handsome, athletic, and intelligent, and I was a sucker for red heads. I was instantly attracted to him and he adored me. He was emotionally strong and seemed to be able to handle anything and everything. He was ambitious, hardworking, and he loved to have a good time. He was decisive, organized, disciplined, and he knew what he wanted in life. It was a match made in heaven.

I knew that Jeff would make a wonderful husband and father to our children. He was loyal, honest to a fault, and extremely dedicated. I thought that Jeff and I would live happily ever after with our healthy, beautiful, smart children. Everything would be wonderful and we would be able to sail through any challenges that we faced. I thought that our life together was going to be an extension of the wonderful life to which I was accustomed. I was living in a magnificent bubble. I wasn't ready for the bubble to pop.

There is nothing more difficult than marriage. It's taking two distinct people with completely different backgrounds and bringing them together under one roof for the rest of their lives. Try throwing an extremely sick child into that mix.

We had so much anger bottled up we had difficulty communicating with each other. We blamed each another for our inabilities to cope with the struggles of bringing up Jacob.

Jeff and I handle grief in totally different ways. He locks it up inside and tries to keep his feelings to himself. I need to talk, cry, scream, and let it all out. I want him to share and he wants me to let him have his space. We were trying to change each other rather than to accept each other.

We decided to seek professional help. Two years after Jacob's diagnosis, Jeff and I went to a marriage counsellor. The first time Jeff and I rode the elevator up to the tenth floor of the building where our therapy session was, I had no idea what was going on in Jeff's head. All I knew was I wanted to scream or cry. I really didn't think that anything or anyone could help us. I really thought that our marriage was coming to an end.

The therapist made up a fitting analogy about us. She called me Marcia Brady and Jeff the Lone Ranger. It took us a long time to realize that our house was a happier place when Marcia was allowed to be Marcia, and the Lone Ranger was allowed to be the Lone Ranger.

When Jeff and I were first married, the rabbi who married us gave us a pep talk. He told us that the secret to a great marriage is to give 90 per cent and only take back 10 per cent. The therapist's guidance led to the same advice the rabbi gave us years earlier. Jeff and I started to listen to each other.

We made up lists of what we needed and wanted from the other one. I learned that the things that I was giving Jeff were the things that I needed and not what he wanted. Jeff was giving me what he thought that I needed. The two of us slowly began to listen to each other. We both had to give 90 per cent of the time, and only take 10 per cent. Our marriage became stronger, we became closer and we started to communicate. Of course we still have our difficulties, but the foundation has been rebuilt. Now, when the burdens become too much to bear and our marriage seems to be collapsing, we can go back to that foundation and construct it again brick by brick.

One thing we do have in common is that we love each other and our children. Jacob has given both of us strength—strength that we never knew existed until it was tested to the limit.

We know Jacob won't be with us for the long run. So we try to enjoy every moment we have with him. When people hear about our situation they can't believe we are still together.

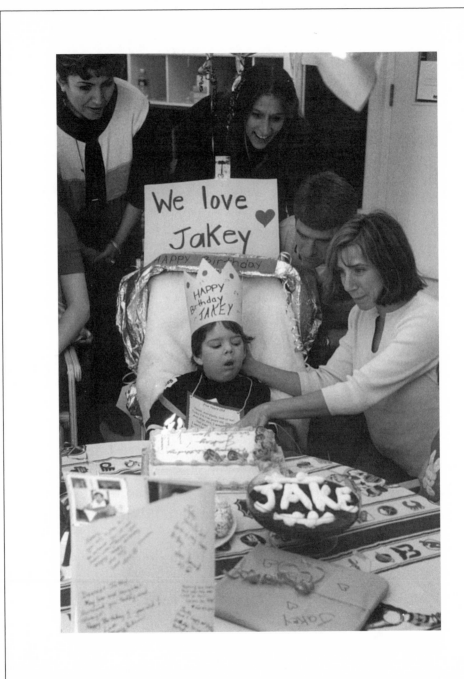

Chapter 5

IN 2002, JACOB TURNED FOUR.

He had turned in to a heavy boy and his medical needs were becoming an issue for Play and Learn. His medications and all of his feeds had to be administered by g-tube, because he had lost his ability to swallow food. Jacob was having difficulty swallowing his own saliva, and he often needed to be suctioned. Jacob needed more individual attention and Play and Learn couldn't accommodate him anymore. The transition from Play and Learn to his new school, Beverley School, was not easy.

As much as we loved Play and Learn, we began searching for other options. I checked out private schools for children with disabilities. While many seemed wonderful they were extremely costly and very far away.

I began to investigate special schools belonging to the public Toronto Board of Education. This was another frustrating experience. Jacob couldn't even set foot inside one of those special schools unless I appeared before the Identification, Placement and Review Committee, and I wasn't allowed to meet the IPRC unless I registered Jacob at the public school in our district. Only after he was registered could Jacob be assessed and labelled as special needs.

So I had to enrol Jacob into the local school just so that they could refuse his registration. Walking up the thirty stairs to enter the school that Jacob would never go to was degrading. The beautiful artwork and creative assignments on display in the hallways that tugged at the heartstrings of other parents felt like a punch in the stomach to me. Jacob would never be able to go to a school like this.

Jacob will never read.

Jacob will never write.

I was outraged that the system was forcing me to go through this painful and unnecessary exercise in self-pity. It felt like someone was dangling something wonderful right in front of my face and telling me that I couldn't have it.

After a home visit from a woman who worked for the board's placement program, we were given our date to be reviewed for the IPRC. All this woman did was look at Jacob, fill out forms and agree with me that Jacob was indeed severely disabled, both physically and mentally. I just felt like saying, "duh," but I kept my composure.

We were presented with a list of schools Jacob could attend. I knew he needed a loving atmosphere with the proper care and stimulation. They sent me to check out Beverley School. Once I toured Beverley, I knew we had arrived. This was the right place for Jacob.

This school doesn't just babysit children with special needs, it stimulates and captivates them. It loves them and lets them feel safe in their environment, and teaches them in ways that don't seem possible. Beverley School is a very special place for very special people.

Located on Baldwin Street in downtown Toronto, the school is hidden in the heart of Chinatown. You drive down a one-way street and in between a church and a small apartment building you notice a peculiar building that looks out of place. The front of the school looks like a massive loading dock that you would find in the shipping department of a factory. It is a loading dock. But instead of freight, it loads and unloads special children in wheelchairs. Handicapped accessible vehicles line up to deliver children with their teachers. That is what I call special delivery.

You enter the wide automatic doors into the grand entrance of the Beverley School. For safety, a low, carpeted wall borders the small accessible playground in the foyer. As you look through the window to the right, you can see the large indoor swimming pool. This room and the pool are both kept at a constant and comfortable ninety degrees, just like a warm bath. Jacob goes swimming once or twice a week at an indoor pool. To Jacob, nothing feels better than being submerged in the warm water. The water bears his weight and suddenly there are no constraints on his limbs.

To the left of the entrance are the doors to the gym. Though it looks just like an regular elementary school gym, once you see the equipment, it's obvious that there is nothing regular about it. All the bars and climbing apparatus are low enough be reached from the floor and the bikes have been specially adapted so children with specific needs can feel the thrill of riding them just like any child.

The three full-time registered nurses hang their coats in the office across from the pool where they go over the medical protocols required for the children who need continuous nursing care. They are armed with medications administered through g-tubes, suction machines, feeding pumps and puffers, or whatever each child needs for survival.

Across from the nurses office is the snoezelen room. This specialized room is no bigger than a large walk-in closet, but for children like Jacob it is like a trip to Disney World. A remote control covered with buttons sits on a table. Press on the right button and two large clear tubes filled with water spring to life. The colour of the water continuously turns from red to purple to blue to green to pink. The water bubbles up and real-looking fish swim and leap through the bubbles.

Press another button and long fibre optic lights spring into action. The children lie on a mat and the warm, soothing lights run through their fingers, toes, and all over their little bodies. A vibrating mat massages their arms, legs, backs, necks, and heads. Other buttons change the music and the mood of the room. These children, always dependent on others, can actually make things happen for themselves.

scooped little bits of whipped cream onto Jacob's lips. We watched as his tongue slowly poked out of his lips to get a taste of the delicious, sweet flavour.

I recalled the literature on survival rates for children with Canavan disease. Most die before the age of four.

Jacob was four. And going strong.

I, ON THE OTHER HAND, WAS THIRTY-SIX IN 2002.

If Jeff and I were going to have any more children it would have to be soon. We were so grateful for Beverly and Jacob that we thought our plates were completely full, and that was it for childbearing. I couldn't face another pregnancy wondering if my baby was going to be healthy.

But with the cloud of Jacob's fate constantly over our heads, Jeff and I wanted another sibling for Beverly because we knew that someday she would lose her big brother. We also knew that life wasn't going to be easy for her with an extremely handicapped brother. She deserved to have someone who could understand her and share her experiences and feelings. When Beverly was two and Jacob was four, I became pregnant again. That year I had two miscarriages within six months of each other. I was completely distraught and believed that our wish for Beverly to have someone else in her family wasn't meant to be.

After my second miscarriage, one of my girlfriends came over. She is religious. I, on the other hand, was not at all—spiritual yes, but religious no. She told me that I was going to the mikvah. At this time, I wasn't really even sure what a mikvah was, or what was involved. She taught me that it is a ritual bath for Orthodox Jewish women that offers a spiritual cleansing. She was certain that if I went, I would become pregnant and stay pregnant. I felt that I had nothing to lose and, that at very least, this would be a learning experience.

A mikvah looks like a large hot tub without the bubbles. Alone in the mikvah room, I slipped off my robe and stepped into the warm, soothing water. A lady came into the room to watch me take my ritual dunks. Each time I went under the water, I said a prayer. After, she left. I stayed in the warm pool and began to sob like a child. I really felt I was close to God. I cried and cried. I couldn't understand why God was giving me such incredible challenges. I wanted answers but none were given. I stayed in this bath until my fingers and toes shrivelled up like prunes. God and I had made peace.

That evening Ben was conceived.

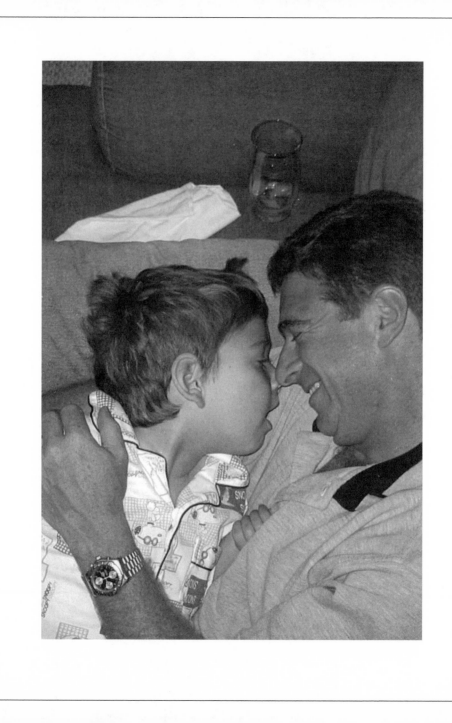

Chapter 6

BY 2003, JACOB'S BIRTHDAYS HAD BECOME LEGENDARY. As May approached, everyone was excited about what we were going to do for Jacob's birthday. I was pregnant, and feeling extremely weak and discouraged because of my two miscarriages in the previous months.

I was in my first trimester but completely exhausted, both physically and mentally, so we told our friends and family that Jacob just wanted some one-on-one time with the special people in his life. When one person is speaking, he can concentrate on that one voice, and that one voice is everything to Jacob. When there are too many voices he isn't able to focus.

Jeff woke Jacob with kisses. Jacob loves Jeff's kisses. My father was the first to arrive that morning. As soon as Jacob heard his tone-deaf voice singing "Happy Birthday," his face lit up.

THE PHONE DIDN'T STOP RINGING THAT DAY. FAMILY members called just to sing into Jacob's ear. Friends, aunts, uncles, and cousins arrived throughout the day, one by one, to share special birthday moments with Jacob. Watching him try to speak to the ones he loves is priceless. He says so much without saying anything at all.

Jacob has a hypnotic effect on people. Once they come in to his life, they never leave. Jacob has two nurses and one personal support worker who rotate shifts over the course of the week. Usually this type of help is extremely difficult to find, but somehow these women have remained loyal to Jacob and have been working with him for over four years.

They don't just sit with Jacob. They treat him as if he were their own. When they bathe him they don't just clean him up, they play with him in the shower and sing him songs. When they take him out for strolls, they take extra care to make sure that he has an extra blanket if it is cold outside, and they bring along books so they can break at a park bench, cuddle up to read to him. Extra care is given when they exercise his limbs. One of the nurses even made Jacob handcrafted mat covers and face wipes. These women are so dedicated to Jacob that they have become part of our family.

I teach grade four. Jacob has become a major part of my curriculum. My students are learning life lessons that I wish I could have learned. I feel blessed and honoured to be able to enrich children with these lessons. These are the lessons of sympathy, empathy, open-mindedness, and acceptance.

I'm not the type of teacher who can separate my personal life from my work. I bring the classroom home, and my home to the classroom. My students are invited to my house to spend time with Jacob. Some of them read him stories, some play musical instruments, and others just sit and talk. Others push Jacob around the block in his wheelchair and take him for rides on his hospital bed by pushing the buttons to make the bed ascend or descend. Whatever they do, when they leave my house they are changed forever.

I often bring Jacob to school as well. We place him on an exercise mat at the front of the classroom and the students take turns sitting beside him and holding his hand. They know that if they have a cold they aren't able to visit with Jacob that day and they completely respect that. Some of them help me give him his medication by g-tube. They think that it is so cool that he doesn't have to eat vegetables or taste disgusting medicine. At recess, they push him around the schoolyard and play with him as if he was one of the gang.

I asked my grade four class to write down the lessons Jacob has taught them. Here are some of their answers:

"Jacob has taught me that even if you have a problem in life, you should be happy and enjoy it while you can."

"I've been taught by Jacob to not be afraid of sick people."

"He is a child like everybody else. He enjoys everything so much. He has taught me to enjoy life and go on with the bad things."

One mother wrote this letter that was published in the school newspaper: "Our daughter's teacher brings an added bonus to the class by exposing them to life outside the classroom with the trials and triumphs of her son's illness, and has lit within her students a spark of compassion and strength in times of challenge which no textbook could teach them."

Jacob allows others to feel comfortable around people who are different. When they come face to face with somebody who is extremely handicapped they are now more likely smile a genuine smile rather than to do whatever they can to uncomfortably look the other way.

Chapter 7

MAY 17, 2004 WAS A SUNNY AND WARM SPRING-LIKE day. Rays of light were shining through the treetops. Jacob was swinging in his blue reclining swing as the children from the street ran around the backyard.

Jacob is six. His sister Bev had turned four, and Ben was one.

When we purchased our home, Jeff and I made a choice. It was either furniture or a playground in the backyard for our children. We knew that it would be difficult to bring Jacob to the park, so why not bring the park to Jacob?

With three swings and hanging rings, our backyard park runs from one end of the yard to the other, and Beverly, Ben and Jacob can swing together. Jacob's swing is next to a two-storey fort where children climb up on the ladders and ropes like mountain climbers. The neighbourhood mountaineers glide down the long, steep slide that extends to the other end of the tree house and to the ground.

In the winter, Jeff turns the backyard into a skating rink. He laces on his skates and tows his son in his plastic sled. The rink and the playground bring the children out and into Jacob's life.

The children on the street love our backyard. What's better than a park with a private bathroom and room service? Jacob listens to the laughter as the children run and jump and climb. The warm sun against his skin and the light brush of a breeze on his face make Jacob smile from ear to ear. A simple pleasure for us is everything for Jacob.

When most families go on family outings, they grab a couple of diapers, some snacks, a sippy cup, and off they go. Getting out of the house for a family outing is a little more difficult in our household.

Here's the drill. First, we get Beverly and Ben ready and put their stuff in a knapsack by the front door. We prepare Jacob's medications for the amount of time we will be away. Some of his meds have to be kept cold and others kept at room temperature. They are all measured and poured into syringes for quick and easy use as needed. Then we prepare Jacob's food by opening a can of Peptamen Junior, a nourishing meal supplement, and pouring it into his enteral feeding container attached to his portable pump, which is attached to Jacob's feeding tube in his stomach. Then we grab his portable suction machine. And finally we are ready to dress the children.

Inside, coats, boots, snow pants, hats, and gloves are laid out in different areas of the family room. While one of us dresses the children, the other one loads the car. In goes the knapsack with Jacob's paraphernalia. Then we set up Jacob's special car seat and Jacob's wheelchair is manually lifted into the back of the van.

One of us dresses Ben and then Jacob. His limbs are extremely stiff and at it's very hard to manoeuvre his arms through the holes of his jacket sleeves. Thank goodness Beverly is self-sufficient.

One of us carries Jacob to the car in a fireman's carry. We buckle everyone in and one of us waits in the car with the kids while the other one cleans up the mess we left inside. And off we go. Covered in sweat and completely exhausted, we can begin our day.

MOST PEOPLE WAKE UP TO THE SOUND OF AN ALARM clock.

Our alarm clock is Jacob, and Jacob doesn't come with a snooze button. We can never anticipate what we will hear in the morning. Will Jacob be coughing? Will he be vocalizing? Will he be giggling? We can't anticipate when our morning will begin. Will it be 4 AM, 5 AM, 6 AM, 7 AM? When I give Jacob his second dose of sleep medication the evening before, I am always hoping that he will sleep through the night.

The reality is that Jacob usually wakes up in the middle of the night at some point and he'll be coughing. One of us goes downstairs to make sure he's okay. Jeff and I alternate nights just so that one of us can have the chance to get some undisturbed sleep until morning. We'll turn him, change his diaper and give him an injection of chloral hydrate. We are woken up for sure once a night, sometimes twice.

No matter how rough the night before was, the day must still go on. Ben wakes us up between 6 and 7 AM and then our day really begins. At this point all I really want to do is crawl back into bed. Ben and I climb downstairs, quickly checking on Jacob just to make sure that he is resting peacefully. I heat up some milk for Ben, and make some coffee for me. The two of us cuddle on the couch, our time together, and watch *Dora the Explorer* until it is time to wake Jacob.

Our nanny comes upstairs at 7:30 AM and the morning rush hour starts. Jacob gets picked up for school at 8 AM sharp and there is a lot of work to be done to be sure he is ready. We wake him up, change his diaper, and unplug his g-tube, which feeds him all night long while he sleeps.

One of us dresses Jacob while the other wakes Beverly. Jacob doesn't like to be dressed because his arms and legs are so stiff and it hurts when we put his arms into the sleeves of his shirt no matter how careful we are.

Usually we have to suction Jacob in the morning because he gets so congested overnight. He coughs and we run to him carrying the suction machine just hoping to catch the mucus in time. The suction machine is basically a vacuum, kind of like what you find in a dentist's office, and is used to help Jacob get rid of his secretions. The children don't even notice the piercing sound of the suction machine anymore. It's just part of the routine.

Jacob sits in his special chair positioned on the sofa. It looks like a large car booster seat, but in a reclining position. We had a terrycloth cover made for Jacob's chair with a Toronto Maple Leafs motif. Beverly and Ben sit beside Jacob, in the family room there eating their breakfast and watching their show on television.

Meanwhile, Jacob's teeth are brushed and his mouth is suctioned. His face is wiped and Blistex is applied to his lips. His meds are drawn and given to him right before his bus arrives at 8 AM. Jacob has to take medication every four hours for pain management. He takes Tylenol, which is crushed and mixed with water, so it can be easily delivered by g-tube. His Losec is also taken the same way. Jacob suffers from acid reflux and Losec prevents the productions of acid in the stomach. He also takes nitrazepam, an anti-epileptic drug that helps control seizure activity, and baclofen to stop muscle spasms. He gets his drugs at just before 8 AM, then at noon, then at 4 PM, and once more at 8 PM

Everyone sits in the family room for breakfast. Beverly and Ben eat at the coffee table because I like having all my children together in the same room and Jacob isn't able to sit at the kitchen table. Jacob is still full from his evening meal, but he likes to keep his brother and sister company. When it's close to eight, we slip on Jacob's coat, hat, booties, and gloves, and carry him to his wheelchair waiting for him outside. If I have time, I rush upstairs, brush my teeth, comb my hair, throw on some clothes, and hurry back down so I can carry

Jacob outside to his wheelchair without showing the world my flannel pyjamas.

At eight o'clock, the doorbell rings and Marylou, a registered nurse, is ready to accompany Jacob on his forty-five-minute commute to Beverly School. I give her Jacob's suction machine, his meds, and his feeding pump. I wheel him to the van, give him a kiss, and tell him how much I love him. Then they are off.

When Jacob is at school, I don't worry about him. I know that he is loved, stimulated, and having the best time. If there is a problem, his teacher calls me immediately.

Then I finish dressing Ben and Bev and off we go to school.

Jacob is delivered back home by 3 PM One of his nurses greets him and, with the assistance of our nanny, they carry Jacob inside and unhooked him from his feeding pump. He is stretched out on his mat because he is stiff from the forty-five-minute van ride home. His diaper is changed, and Jacob can relax from his very busy day at school. His nurse caregiver massages him and stretches out all of his limbs while he hangs out with Beverly and Ben. On go his orthotics, leg braces that support his joints and limbs to keep his feet in a bent position. Without them Jacob's feet will become so stiff that they are almost pointed like a ballerina's, *en pointe*. These orthotics help stretch his joints and muscles. You've heard the expression "what you don't use, you lose"? Well, Jacob can't use his feet so they are losing their shape.

By the time I get home from work at 4:30, the house is filled with laughter and Jacob is surrounded by the commotion and excitement of neighbourhood children and nannies. I love coming home to a busy and active house.

Because of Jacob's love of music, our playroom is filled with musical toys with big buttons that he can push to make sounds. Sometimes we'll lay him backwards on his large exercise ball and roll him backwards and forwards. Other times he will lay face down on the ball and we will bounce him up and down. He just loves the motion and the stretches give him relief. Sometimes I'll lie on the floor and give him an airplane ride. It's not as easy as it sounds because he weighs so much. I have to work out regularly to keep my stomach muscles and back muscles strong just so I can lift him. Most people work out so that they can stay fit. Jeff and I work out so we can lift our child.

I make supper to the sounds of children playing and at times arguing. Nothing can be better.

Jeff comes home around six and Beverly and Ben run into his arms. As soon as Jacob hears the door slam and his daddy calls, "Hello, anybody home?" Jacob's eyes light up. Jacob hears him say, "Where's Jacob," and a gigantic smile covers his face.

While Jeff, Beverly, Ben, and I eat supper, Jacob is showered and changed into his pyjamas by his nurse. After supper, we bathe Beverly and Ben, watch television, chat about our day, and enjoy each other's company.

We put Ben and Beverly to bed at about eight o'clock and while one of us is upstairs with them, Jacob will be vocalizing "Ahhhhh!" The sound of joy will resound from downstairs as he calls out. Sometimes his happiness is so loud it keeps our other children from falling asleep. At times we have to shut the doors to the family room because he is so loud.

Jacob speaks to us in his very own language. He tells us in his own words how happy and content he feels. His timing may be a little off, but who cares if Jacob is happy.

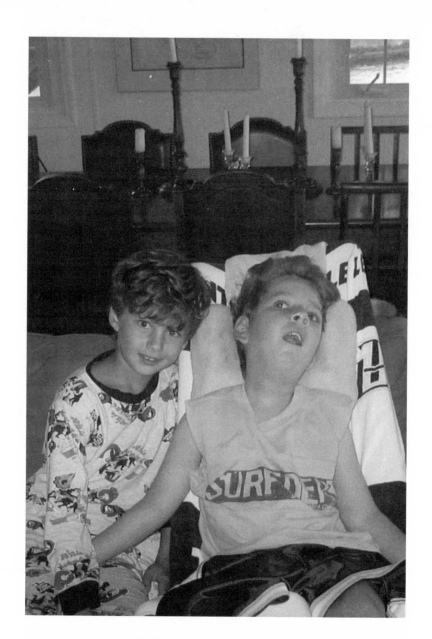

Jacob with his cousin Dylan Levy.

Chapter 8

JACOB'S SEVENTH BIRTHDAY WAS HELD AT HIS FAVOURITE place: Beverley School. We wanted him to be able to share his school world with his cousins, aunts, uncles, and grandparents.

The principal at Beverley obliged by arranging to open the school for our family on a Saturday. The caretaker, Mario, gave up a day from his precious weekend and brought his family as guests to Jacob's birthday party. The school arranged for the lifeguards to come in so Jacob could swim with his family and friends.

Mario opened the gym and put out hula hoops and balls and bicycles of all sizes. Jacob's brother and sister and cousins ran around the gym throwing balls into the baskets and playing with all the equipment. They were having the best time. They couldn't believe that Jacob was able to come here everyday and thought he was so lucky.

The caretaker opened the snoezelen room with its special lights and soft, soothing music so Jacob's cousins could feel its magic. The lifeguards put out the swimming gear so that everyone could climb into the warm, relaxing water and slide, and jump, and swim with Jacob. His favourite tunes blared from the school's loudspeakers.

Even Jacob's teachers came to help him celebrate his special day. One of his favourite teachers gave him a special present—chocolate-flavoured lip balm. "Watch this," she said. She bent close to Jacob and asked, "Jacob, would you like some chocolate?" His tongue jutted out of his mouth. She applied the lip balm to his lips. She asked again, "Jacob, would you like some more chocolate?" Again, he did the same thing.

She had made a connection with Jacob. He was communicating with her. He knew exactly what she was saying. He wanted to taste the chocolate and he knew how to ask for more.

I have described the importance for Jacob of a safe place, a place where no one can hurt him and he can feel completely at home and safe. For me, one of those places is our family cottage. Whenever I drive in and see the lake, wonderful memories from my childhood flood my brain and I feel inner peace and freedom.

When my brothers and I were little, my parents used to pack the cars in June and up we'd go. My brothers and I would spend two full months playing with our cousins, running around in the fresh north air and swimming in Lake Simcoe. We spent our days swimming, canoeing, waterskiing, sailing, windsurfing, boating, and playing in the sand.

We wouldn't see city life until Labour Day.

Now my children, including Jacob, are lucky enough to share similar experiences. Watching my children have the same adventures that I had as a child is even more special to me than my own memories.

There is nothing better than sitting outside with my brothers and their families watching our children play together. Beverly does handstands in the water while her cousins swim around her. Ben makes sandcastles in the sand with help from his older cousins. And Jacob lies in his special blow-up raft listening to the sounds of fun that surround him and breathing in the warm country air.

My brothers will bring out their guitars and serenade Jacob with hits from the sixties and seventies while my sister-in-law plunks herself next to Jacob and sings especially for him. Jacob smiles from ear to ear and at times it seems he even tries to sing along.

Sometimes I look around and feel sadness because Jacob isn't able to play with his cousins the way kids are supposed to. He is the oldest and the others would have looked up to him if everything were normal. But I snap out of it pretty quickly and enjoy the moment.

I once said to Jacob's six-year-old cousin, Dylan, "Do you realize that if Jacob was healthy the two of you would be best friends?"

"Jacob is my best friend," he replied.

JACOB CAN BRIGHTEN UP ANYONE'S DAY, EVEN WHEN a judge is determined to have order in his court. In February 2004, Jacob and I got a parking ticket on the coldest day of the year. The wind was roaring and snow was falling hard but I needed to run in to pick up my eyeglasses. I had Jacob with me in the car so I parked my car in a handicapped zone, and wheeled Jacob into the building. Five minutes later we came out to the car only to find a seventy-five-dollar parking ticket. I couldn't believe that the police officer didn't notice the wheelchair sign just under the windshield on the passenger side of the van.

I was furious.

Of course, I decided to fight the ticket. Two months later, Jacob and I went to court. As I was strolling Jacob in his chair down the hall to find the courtroom, a police-woman came up to us and said, "Please tell me that you aren't here because of me?"

I showed her the ticket and she explained to me that the place that I parked was a drop-off zone for special needs. You aren't allowed to park there, you can only drop people off. I shrugged my shoulders and looked at her. She completely understood what I was saying without a word being said.

The officer told me that she would try to speak to the judge about the offence when we were called up in court, but we would still have to go through with the trial.

I had never been to court before, and it was definitely Jacob's first time. When the grand doors opened everyone presented their tickets to the court clerk. I was the tenth person in line. The judge sat down sternly and asked for silence in the courtroom. You could have heard a pin drop.

Suddenly Jacob got the giggles. He thought that the silence was absolutely hilarious. The judge asked me to stand up and ordered me to control my child. I couldn't possibly, and I was smiling. I'm not sure if it was because I felt like I was a schoolgirl in trouble with the principal or because Jacob was cracking me up. The judge asked the clerk to find our file immediately. I thought that we were in real trouble. Instead, the judge dismissed the case right away. The judge gave us a little smile and told us to have a great day.

Chapter 9

BY MAY 17, 2005, JACOB WEIGHED FIFTY-FIVE POUNDS.

Lifting him up and down a flight of stairs is extremely difficult, not to mention dangerous. He can't help, and his weight is unevenly distributed, like a sack of potatoes. Jeff and I work out not because we want to remain trim but so that we can carry our son without breaking our backs. As Jacob gets heavier, we become stronger and fitter.

Watching Jacob's nurses and his nanny lift him up and down the stairs made us extremely nervous. What if they fall? What if they slip? When his nanny lifts Jacob, his feet almost touch the floor. Something had to be done.

Some Canavan children die before the age of four.

Jacob had defied the odds. He had lived two lifetimes. Who was to say he wouldn't outlive me or his father?

Not me.

For his eighth birthday we decided that Jacob needed a new room. Careful preparation went into planning his special room, which was once the dining room on the main level of our house.

We had investigated installing an elevator so Jacob could sleep on the same floor as the rest of us. The amount of money we would have needed to spend was extraordinary. And it would have only solved one problem. We still would have had to construct a bathroom to meet Jacob's special needs. To bathe Jacob, we have to lift him out of his hospital bed, walk down the hall with him in our arms, straddle the bathtub, and bend down and carefully position him in the tub. It is literally backbreaking.

Lifting him out is even more challenging. We have to bend over the side of the tub, carefully manoeuvre our arms under his neck and knees, and lift a slippery, heavy, no-longer-little boy who is unable to assist in any way. We run all the way back to his room, lay him on his bed and cover him with towels before he freezes.

Jacob's new bedroom changed all that.

Jeff hired a contractor who listened to our story and helped us build Jacob a room that would fit his needs and ours.

We used a third of the former dining room to construct another room that would serve as Jacob's shower. We installed heat lamps so that whenever Jacob takes a shower the room remains toasty warm. The whole Schwartz family could comfortably shower at the same time in Jacob's special bathroom.

We purchased a bath seat with a stand on wheels, basically a glorified miniature lawn chair the same height as

Jacob's bed. We simply slide Jacob from his bed onto the bath seat and roll him into the heated shower. Now bathing him is easy.

The walls of Jacob's new room are covered with mementoes of his past. The collage given to him from his friends at Play and Learn hangs there, and so do framed pictures of Jacob and his friends. His hospital bed is covered with a boyish duvet and matching pillowcases and sheets. His throw pillows are enlarged stuffed balls—a football, a basketball, and a baseball. The shelves are filled with toys and books so that Jacob can play in his room with his brother and sister.

His is the first room you see when you enter the house. With two mirrored doors at the entrance, when the doors are shut, the front hall looks just like every one else's. One would assume that behind those elegant doors you would find an elegant dining room matching the rest of the home's decor.

When Jacob is ill and bedridden we can close off his room to give him the privacy he needs. Most days those doors are kept open so that everyone who enters our home knows that someone special lives here.

JACOB'S FIRST NIGHT IN HIS NEW ROOM WAS difficult for me. Even though he was just downstairs I felt like I had sent my son to overnight camp for the first time. It felt so lonely without him upstairs with the rest of us. I had this overwhelming feeling of guilt and regret. I wanted him to be with all of us, like all of us.

The first night I spent two hours crying myself to sleep. We spent all of the time and money building this perfect room for Jacob and I wanted it to go away. I hated the fact that while everyone was sleeping peacefully upstairs Jacob seemed so far away.

Each night became easier, and each morning became more manageable. Everything is accessible, so dressing Jacob and getting him ready for school is a relative snap because he is downstairs already.

Jacob is eight. His new room is one birthday present Jacob will enjoy every day for the rest of his life.

THERE ARE MANY REASONS TO CELEBRATE AND MANY special days. Chanukah is a celebration of eight nights representing a miracle that happened thousands of years ago.

We celebrated our miracle at our family Chanukah party. Jeff put dabs of chocolate icing on Jacob's bottom lip and Jacob kept thrusting out his tongue to have just a little taste.

He loved the sounds of his cousins ripping open their presents. Jacob nestled in his grandfather's strong arms laughing and smiling and loving every second. Watching my father look at Jacob with love is a gift. He was so proud of his little Jacob, a little boy who was not supposed to be there.

Our Chanukah miracle is not the eight days that the oil lasted, but the eight incredible years that Jacob's inner light has been shining and sparkling and teaching all of us that miracles do happen.

Some holidays are not as celebratory as planned. It is now 1:30 PM, New Year's Day, and I am sitting inside a luxurious chalet just steps away from the foot of a ski hill. I am looking out the large ten-foot-high windows, watching all the skiers fly down the white slippery slopes, and the families sitting on the chairlifts together. Jeff, Beverly, and Ben are all out enjoying the festivities and programs on the hill.

Jacob hasn't woken up yet. It's not because he partied too hard the night before. Jacob aspirated during the three-hour drive. He coughed and secretions entered his lungs before I could get him on his suction machine. Now he is having difficulty breathing because he isn't able to swallow his secretions quickly enough.

He continues to fight by coughing and throwing up, but his little lungs are all tired out. His body has completely shut down and all he can do is sleep. I am sitting here listening to Jacob's laboured breathing in harmony with his feeding pump whirring continuously.

Jeff can't enjoy his special time with the other two children because he is worrying about Jacob. He is on the slopes and I am sitting inside but there are plenty of times when the tables are turned.

We both know that Jacob will break out of this because, in our household, this is routine. This is just a day in the life of Jacob.

One beautiful and memorable day at a time.

Chapter 10

JACOB HAS NOT ONLY CHANGED MY LIFE, HE HAS CHANGED the lives of everyone in our household. He has changed the lives of our family members, our extended family, our friends, our community and he continues to touch the lives of millions of people.

Years ago, when Jacob was just one, we were emotionally preparing ourselves and Jacob for the gene-replacement trial, Jeff and I knew that we didn't want any other family to have to go through anything like this. Jacob's enrolment in the trial was groundbreaking news. Our story was featured in Toronto newspapers and news broadcasts. Jacob was one of sixteen children in the world enrolled in this radical experimental gene-replacement trial. If this procedure proved successful, it could have been a mammoth step toward developing cures for neurodegenerative illnesses.

It just so happened that a barista from our local Starbucks recognized Jacob and me on television and told his manager our story. The next day after the newscast, Jacob and I strolled to that same Starbucks for my grande, sugar-free, vanilla, Lactaid latte. I received much more than a latte that day.

The manager explained that their cafe wanted to help us raise money for the trial at Yale. I was flabbergasted. I couldn't believe strangers wanted to help us. I ran home to call Jeff to tell him this incredible news.

As overwhelmed as we were by Starbucks' generosity, Jeff and I felt uncomfortable accepting money on our own behalf. We didn't want the money to go directly to Jacob, because we were too proud. However, we definitely wanted to raise money to help fund the research.

We decided to develop a charitable organization so that other parents wouldn't have to go through what we were going through. We wanted people to know that Canavan disease existed. We didn't want to see another child born with such a debilitating, progressive, and deadly disease because at the time screening was unavailable and unknown in Canada. We wanted Jacob's life to serve a purpose. We wanted this charity to become a legacy for our son.

WE TOLD OUR FAMILY AND FRIENDS ABOUT THE Starbucks offer and asked them to help us launch a charitable organization in Jacob's name. My brother came up with the name Jacob's Ladder. We loved the connotation of climbing the ladder to find a cure, not to mention the beautiful biblical story of Jacob reaching heaven: "And Jacob dreamed, and behold a ladder set up on the earth, and the top of it reached to heaven: and behold the angels of God as ending and descending on it."

The name was a perfect fit.

Starbucks' employees canvassed the stores and restaurants in our neighbourhood for prizes and gift certificates. Hundreds of people came out. Starbucks raised over ten thousand dollars.

Jacob's Ladder was born.

Little did we know that this charity launched through our local Starbucks' inspiration, would develop into a million-dollar foundation funding research into neurodegenerative diseases, to encourage genetic screening for parents, and parents-to-be, as well as to sponsor international prizes in the area of genetics. Because of Jacob, Jacob's Ladder, Canadian Foundation for the Control of Neurodegenerative Disease, was established in 1998.

In just eight years, it has exceeded all our expectations. As a direct result of our initiatives, parents at risk in Ontario and Vancouver can now be screened for Canavan disease at no cost, and this disease could be eradicated through prevention. It is possible to tell with over 95 per cent certainty whether one or both parents is a carrier.

Genetic counselling is important to assist at-risk couples explore their family-planning options. We have aligned ourselves with the National Tay-Sachs and Allied Diseases, Dysautonomia Foundation and the National Council of Jewish Women of Canada to raise awareness of rare genetic disorders and the testing that is now available. A community outreach program to raise public awareness of the screening program was put together with the support of Jacob's Ladder and these other organizations.

We have collaborated with the Hospital for Sick Children Research Institute in Toronto to create a program that provides funding for innovative research for new doctors to make their mark in the study of neurodegenerative diseases. This type of research is not readily funded by many charities, but this is where the breakthroughs come. Jacob's Ladder has pledged $350,000 to create a pilot program. Jacob's Ladder has directed $100,000 of those funds to the Norman Saunders Initiative in Complex Care, a program at Sick Kids dedicated to advancing the care of medically complex children with special health care needs. Dr. Saunders is Jacob's pediatrician and dear friend.

Jacob's Ladder also presents grants to doctors around the world who have made strides in genetics. Grant recipients have come from Baylor College of Medicine in Texas, Harvard University, Oxford University, and Johns Hopkins University where they have achieved a better understanding of autism, Rette syndrome, stem-cell research, and Gaucher's disease.

In 2005, Dr. Hugo Moser, a professor of neurology and pediatrics at Johns Hopkins and the director of the Neurogenetics Research Center at the Kennedy Krieger Institute, was recognized for his work with adrenoleukodystrophy (ALD), a disease that occurs in boys between the ages of four and eight. Boys can recover if they are treated with Lorenzo's oil, celebrated in the movie with the same name. When he accepted the award, Dr. Moser was overwhelmed. "When I was presented with this award, all I had to do was look at my predecessors and I accepted it very quickly," he stated.

Jacob's Ladder also supports a post-doctoral fellowship at Toronto's Hospital for Sick Children. The 2003–2004 fellowship of one hundred thousand dollars was awarded to Dr. Jessie Cameron, who is researching the causes of Leigh's disease. This disease is a progressive neurodegenerative illness similar to Canavan's. Unlike Canavan's, which is easily identified, Leigh's disease is more difficult to diagnose because it can be associated with a deficiency in several different genes. Results of this research may apply to other neurodegenerative diseases such as Parkinson's and Alzheimer's.

Jacob's Ladder is a labour of love. It has put on movie nights, golf tournaments, concerts, screenings, children's family fun days, and has been fortunate enough to be the recipient of support from other organizations that have chosen to direct their fundraising efforts towards Jacob's Ladder's projects, including in 2004 the eBay Foundation.

Jacob's story has inspired so many people. We've had doctors, lawyers, and favourite children's entertainers produce exceptional performances to help Jacob's Ladder climb to a cure. Kayla puts on a Chanukah concert and party each year.

A group of very talented health care professionals presented a show called *Life Beat*. Osgoode Hall law students put on their annual Mock Trial.

In celebration of their fifteenth anniversary, a restaurant called Grazie just published a cookbook. It is sold in bookstores across Canada with partial proceeds go to Jacob's Ladder.

Many children have also contributed to helping Jacob's Ladder. I often open our front door and look down to greet a blushing child grasping a baggie filled with change that he or she had collected. Each one of these children has spent hours of their day selling lemonade that they had made themselves.

The Hillcrest Climb-a-thon raised almost ten thousand dollars. Three hundred preschoolers collected pledges for a special little boy who they call Jacob's Ladder. We drove into the Hillcrest driveway and spotted this humungous, colourful Jacob's Ladder sign created by the children and the schoolyard transformed into a miraculous playground covered with handmade posters, pictures, and sidewalk paintings featuring colourful ladders everywhere. The children were all waiting for Jacob of Jacob's Ladder to appear. We felt like parents of the hippest rock star, and our son's name was up in lights.

Jacob's Ladder has held three extremely successful Family Fun Days when thousands come to celebrate. The committee gathers in the Schwartz family room to brainstorm wonderful original ideas. Jacob lies on his mat in the centre of the room and inspires everyone around him.

The third Jacob's Ladder Family Fun Day, held in December 2005, attracted over 1,500 people with support from sponsors like Scotiabank, Starbucks, TD Securities, Mastermind Educational Toys, Spinmaster, Sandylion Stickers, St. Joseph Thorn Press, Franklin Templeton Investments, Help We've Got Kids, Mint Entertainment, Goodmans LLP, Cinram, GAP, Boiler and Inspection Insurance Company of Canada, Harvey Kalles Real Estate, Forest Hill Real Estate, Chapters and Indigo, Maple Pictures, Coca-Cola, Loots, Mad Science, Pizza Pizza, Sony PlayStation, TicketKing, Mirvish Productions, Second City, Scholastic, Borden Communications, Freed Development, Onroad Communications, Careful Delivery Services, Creative Planning, Quality Meat Packagers, *Today's Parent*, and the Carlu.

Not only did these companies donate money, many of their employees volunteered and participated. Entertainers dedicated their entire day to perform for the crowds of children and families who came out to support Jacob's Ladder.

When you walked off the elevators into the magnificent Carlu in downtown Toronto at the event, all you saw was happiness. More than two hundred volunteers wearing bright red Jacob's Ladder T-shirts welcomed the children and parents with enormous smiles. These volunteers offered their free time to help Jacob climb to a cure. They welcomed the children and their parents with enormous smiles and kindness.

Each room had its own theme, dedicated to children of all ages. Some had their nails manicured in the SpinMaster Spa. Others had their make up done in Barbie's Dress-up Tea Party.

After the children were all dolled up, off they went to play the games. Each sponsor had its own carnival game set up like the Mastermind Shuffle, Cinram Milk Can Toss, TD Securities First and Ten, Exclusive Affair Rental Tip and Troll, Goodmans' Duck Pond, Freed Development Slap Shot, GAP Tic-Tac-Toe, and the Carlu Wheel of Fun.

Everywhere you looked you saw children running around with massive Mastermind Educational shopping bags filled with wonderful prizes and toys. They could buy whatever they wanted for a fraction of the retail cost at the massive Pay-Whatever-You-Want Store, sponsored by Spinmaster Toys and Sandylion Stickers.

The school at which I teach has a program called Project Giveback that teaches the children to understand that wonderful things can happen from tragedy. I try to teach my students about the fulfillment and satisfaction that I get from Jacob's Ladder. Each nine-year-old chooses a charity close to his or her heart. They each plan a fundraiser for their charity and have organized art lessons, dance classes, mini-Olympics, pyjama parties, and magic shows. After the fundraisers, the children write formal business letters to their charities explaining what they had done, and enclosing the money raised. I can't even begin to describe the joy on their faces when they show me the letters of appreciation. Four of my former students asked if they could help Jacob's Ladder find a cure. They set up a stunning booth displaying beaded bracelets and earrings that they had made themselves over the past six months. They sold five-hundred-dollars' worth and gave it all to Jacob's Ladder.

Every room at the Carlu was filled with laughter, jumping children, and entertainers. Starbucks volunteers walked around with trays giving out lattes and hot chocolate.

Suddenly, Kayla's voice resonated over the loud speaker. She asked everyone, all fifteen hundred children in attendance, my family, Jeff, and me to come into the grand theatre, we called Jacob's Lounge. They asked Jeff, Beverly, Ben, and me to come up on stage. I couldn't find Jacob, but soon realized that they had arranged his wheelchair to be secretly hoisted up on stage. They wheeled him to be with us.

Standing beside us at the microphone stood Jacob's two favourite singers: Kayla and my sister-in-law Jennifer. It was a moment I will never forget. They sang this original song for him:

> One heart, one soul, a guiding light
> Not a word need spoken, not a step need take
> Look what a difference

One brave boy can make.
Playing games, singing songs
Spreading love and joy
Climbing a ladder to a cure
For one special, little boy.

His laughter is contagious
His smile is so bright
An inspiration to us all
He truly is a shining light.

Jacob, Jacob
Guiding us in his own way
Jacob, Jacob
Shows us what really matters each day

THERE WASN'T A DRY EYE IN THE ROOM! IT WAS SO beautiful and everyone—children, parents, volunteers, sponsors—felt the magic in the Carlu. People were saying how lucky they were to be there.

Our family members, neighbours and friends were unpacking tractor-trailers loaded with toys at 4 AM. Some of the same people were still there at 7 PM cleaning up.

When I think back at all of the people who gave of themselves that day, I am in awe that so much kindness exists. We witnessed the community coming together one more time selflessly for one special boy.

JACOB HAD MADE A DIFFERENCE.

He teaches everyone. He has reached thousands: toddlers, grade school children, teenagers, and adults. Jacob has created his legacy. I look at my little Jacob sitting frozen in his wheelchair and wonder if he realizes the impact that he has had on the world around him.

"This is for you, buddy. Look what you have done. You are my hero."

Chapter 11

I'VE BEEN FORCED TO COPE WITH ADVERSITY ON A daily basis. People who know me and know all about my daily life always ask, "How do you do it? How do you walk around like everything is rosy? Why are you always smiling? How do you carry on your daily life, raise three children (one of whom has exceptional needs), teach grade four, help run a successful charity, and put dinner on the table every night?"

I happen to have a wonderful husband who takes turns with me in the wee hours of the night. I have an incredible family who will drop anything to help us out, whether it be bringing supper when Jacob is in the hospital, or showing up and volunteering at every Jacob's Ladder event. We have the most fantastic friends who are always there for us, no matter what the issue or problem. We have the most wonderful support workers and loving nurses who come to give us respite help.

Those wonderful people definitely help out with the physical side of things, but the emotional side is a little more complicated.

I learned a valuable lesson from a two-year-old, my own two-year-old. My daughter Beverly was born with a massive hemangioma (strawberry birthmark) on her forehead. It was about the size of a loony, protruded about one inch, and was bright red.

Everywhere we went people stared at her. I would walk along Eglinton Avenue, pulling a wagon, with Jacob lying in the wagon, and Beverly sitting in the caboose. Strangers would look at Jacob, then at Bevy, then at Jacob, then at Bevy, and then they would look at me, they would tilt their heads and give me this look of pity: "You poor, poor woman."

My Bev would look at them and give them the biggest, brightest smile. Immediately, I saw her put people at ease. Whenever anyone wanted to know what that strange phenomenon was on her forehead, she would just look at them as proudly as could be and she would say, "It's my strawberry, It's very, very, pretty."

She believed every word. She thought that she was the most beautiful person in the whole wide world.

We did remove her hemangioma. Six months after her surgery, we bumped into her surgeon. She couldn't take her eyes off of him. Finally, he said, "Beverly, is everything okay?"

She looked at him sadly, and asked him where her strawberry was. She had thought that he loved them so much that he took them and put them on his own forehead. He told her that she was too old to have strawberries, and it was time to give them to another child. She was definitely okay with that answer.

This example illustrates the power that we have to turn any situation into the most positive experience possible.

THERE ARE DAYS, AND I HAVE MANY, WHEN I AM SO angry because I can't find my car keys. I stomp around the house yelling at everyone in my path because, of course, it is always their fault. When I find my keys and I am finally driving to where I want to go, however, I always start to giggle. This day must be amazing because I let myself get so upset about something as silly as this. I am normal. It's okay. I guess things aren't that bad.

Jacob has taught us the true meaning of life: enjoy it while you're here. I find that as long as I enjoy it most of the time, I'm ahead of the game.

❀ ❀ ❀

HOW CAN YOU ENJOY LIFE MOST OF THE TIME, WHEN every day you are living the unknown? Well, first of all, we're all living the unknown, but Jacob's destiny is inevitable. We know that our time is limited with him, so we try to enjoy every lasting moment.

I have learned many tricks that help get me through those bad days when losing your keys is nothing. Those days when you have been up all night, and you have to be the perfect parent, the understanding spouse, the caring friend, the greatest at your job, and still tend to your own needs, when sleep is not an option.

I used to jog down Avenue Road for my shift, when Jacob was in the hospital for three months. I can remember jogging down with tears streaming down my cheeks. I would let so many emotions out that by the time I got down to the hospital I could deal with the situation.

I thank my little Jacob for giving me the inspiration to learn, to strive to be the best person I can be, and for allowing me to be his mother.

In thirty-six years, I have probably had over fifty teachers. I have never had a teacher who has taught me more about life and living than my son.

Jacob has shown me the merit in the expression "We plan and God laughs". He made me realize that I have to take responsibility for my own happiness and my self-worth. Jacob enjoys his life, why can't I enjoy mine? I only have one life as Ellen Schwartz, and I am determined to enjoy it.

If I walk around bitter and full of pity, I would be getting absolutely nothing out of life. Most of my days are enjoyable and fulfilling. I have learned to cope. I am continually changing and adapting everything that I had originally planned. I know now that living in the moment is the only way to live.

Let me tell you the lessons that Jacob has taught me that get me through every day. Some things are so beyond our control and these lessons allow me to control what I can control—my own emotions and actions:

Worry Time

I used to spend all of my time worrying. Not anymore. My mind would be so filled with worries I never had time to properly complete anything. I couldn't escape my own disturbing thoughts. I drove myself crazy asking myself, "Will Jacob ever get better? How am I going to handle this? What can I do? Who can I call? Where can Jeff and I turn to for help? When is life going to become easier? Why me?"

This is what I learned. I was spending way too much time worrying about things that were out of my control. Now I only worry about things that I can control. Every day I set aside a specific time aside to worry. For me, it is shower time. I get into the shower and I worry. I worry and I worry and I worry. I worry about everything and anything that is clogging my brain. It doesn't matter how insignificant. If it bothers me, it's worth worrying time. I think about everything that is taking up valuable space in my brain.

Sometimes I take really long showers, and other days my showers are extremely brief because I have everything under control.

It doesn't matter how insignificant the worry is. If something is bothering me, I worry about it. I have cried in the shower, laughed in the shower, yelled in the shower, and practised saying what I want to say in the shower. Worry time is just that: a specific time scheduled into your day reserved for worrying. After my designated worrying time, if the worries are controllable, I take care of them immediately. If I don't have the time to address my worries immediately, I write them down and make sure that I take care of them before the day ends. I had to develop this skill or I would never have been able to cope with the direction my life had taken.

Now here's the catch. Once the worrying time is over, it's over. If I can control some of the worries, I take care of them right away. I phone Jeff and apologize for my behaviour. I call my friend and apologize. I call my mother and ask her to pick my daughter up after school. I call my student's parent and discuss the problems that she is having in class. I make the shopping list. I book that appointment. Whatever the problem is, if I can take care of it, I do.

If the things that are worrying me are out of my control, I stop worrying about them for the rest of that day. Of course, those thoughts constantly creep back. This is where the skill comes in. I say to myself, "Ellen, you have already worried long and hard about this today. You're going to worry about it tomorrow." Every time I find myself worrying about that same thing, I remind myself that I've worried about that already that day.

If there is nothing that I can do, I don't worry about it any more.

If I catch myself still worrying about that same thing later in the day, I say to myself, "Ellen, you've worried about that already. There's nothing you can do about it. Worry about it tomorrow."

Tomorrow I worry about it again. I worry long and hard, but only for my worry time. When I worried about it enough I move on to my next worry until that particular worry no longer needs such intense attention.

It works. When Jeff and I are having a spat, and just like any other couple we do, I use my worry time to organize my thoughts. When my mother is ill, I use my worrying time to think about how I can help her. When Jacob is sick, I cry and cry. But I know that there is nothing I can do about and I can't spend my whole day dwelling on his disabilities and fragile health.

Worry time is the most important appointment you can keep in the day. It leaves your brain free to enjoy all the little surprises that pop up—the beauty of a morning after a fresh snowfall, the wonderful silence in the middle of the night, the taste of delicious food. Before I developed my worry-time practice, I didn't notice any of the small wonders because I was too busy worrying about the terrible things. Now I can be a person who enjoys life, just like Jacob.

No Expectations

I can't tell you how many times I have been let down by people because I expected them to act a certain way. I used to take note of everyone who didn't come to visit while we were spending day and night at the hospital with Jacob. I was so angry. I couldn't believe that some friends and family members never bothered to call, write, send something, or visit.

I was so busy spending all this energy resenting others that I failed to notice all the people who did call, write, send something, or visit. I learned pretty quickly that if I didn't expect anything I would be pleasantly surprised by the generosity of others. Friends and family brought us meals. Our brothers and sisters took care of Beverly and drove her to her programs. Jeff's brother spent evenings with Jacob in hospital when he knew that we were exhausted. My brother and sister-in-law even gave us money to buy something frivolous that would put a smile on our faces. People were constantly asking us what they could do.

Once I lowered my expectations of others, I was receptive to the goodness in others. I understood what the rabbi meant when told us that if we give 90 per cent and only take 10 per cent, we would be more content. The less we expect the happier and more fulfilled we are.

Jacob expects absolutely nothing, but he is always thrilled with everything he receives. When he is well, just the feeling of a hand on his is comforting. When Jacob hears a hello from a familiar voice, he lights up. When he is serenaded, it's like he is sitting in front row centre at a Rolling Stones concert. Just a kiss to the cheek can make Jacob squeal with delight. One push on a swing is like a massive roller coaster ride for him. It takes almost nothing to make Jacob happy. He expects nothing and everything means everything to him.

Pity Party

There are still mornings when I feel so down that it's a struggle to take my head off of the pillow. Sometimes when I have been up since 2 AM, I can't bear to face the responsibilities of the day.

There are days when I am envious of other people's marriages because Jeff and I can't even sleep in the same room. Jacob wakes us up almost every night between 2 AM and 5 AM One of us always has to get up to allow the other one to sleep. It is the middle of the night, when most people are enjoying a peaceful slumber, and one of us has to change Jacob's diaper, change his position, give him medication through his tube, and listen to the monitor until he has fallen back to sleep before we can drift back into dreamland.

I am envious of other families who can go on vacations. Because of all of Jacob's everyday needs, equipment, and nursing care, this is extremely difficult for us. We aren't prepared to leave him at home either, because he is part of our family and when we go away Jacob comes with us. Like most couples, Jeff and I go through the ups and downs of marriage. We are always exhausted, overwhelmed, and overworked.

Talk about feeling sorry for yourself. I felt ripped off. I had so many questions for God. Why? How could you do this? Why Jacob? Why us? How could anyone do this to a small child? I was so angry, so devastated. Life stopped and I didn't know what to do. I couldn't function for the longest time.

But I knew that this self-destructive behaviour had to stop. I just couldn't feel sorry for myself all the time. I was a wife. I was a mother, a daughter, a sister, a sister-in-law, a teacher, a friend, a person. I had two choices: I could go through life letting all these negative emotions build up inside me, or I could face these challenges head on.

To me, there was only one choice. I had to start living again, but at the same time I had to address the issues that were filling up my insides.

I couldn't speak to my husband or to other family members about my feelings because they were trying to cope with the same issues. I needed to vent. I didn't want to explain myself. I just wanted someone to listen to me.

I called my closest girlfriend. I told her that I needed to blow off some steam and asked her to listen. She was there immediately. She was thrilled to be my sounding board. We walked and I screamed, yelled, and cried, about everything and anything that I was feeling. She held my hand and listened without judgement. I blamed everybody for everything. I made accusations and my friend just listened. I said some things that I knew that I didn't mean, but it felt so good to say them. My girlfriend didn't try to fix things. She didn't offer suggestions or tell me that I was wrong. She listened, and that's all I wanted or needed. Then I asked her to forget everything that I had just confessed.

I need the pity party, or should I say self-pity party, to endure the feelings that can overwhelm me. I love Jacob more than life. He has given me incredible hope and changed me in so many ways. He has created more challenges than I ever thought I would ever have to endure. I have to be his mother. I have to be strong. I have to be resilient, and I have to be loving. He has taught me to deal with my feelings and then move on, because I have a very important job to do. Without the pity parties I couldn't be the mother or wife that I have to be for Jeff, Jacob, Beverly, and Ben.

This pity party made a world of difference to my state of mind. By just being honest, and telling someone else exactly how I feel it helps cure the problem. I soon realize that I am feeling sorry for myself.

From that day on, whenever it is necessary, I plan a pity party. I vent about my marriage, my frustrations about children, family problems, or just life in general.

Me Time

I cannot be good to anyone else unless I am good to myself. Sometimes I go upstairs to my bedroom and shut the door just for ten minutes. I don't just shut the door, I shut out the world. I lie down on my bed, I close my eyes, I breathe, and I relax. When I come downstairs I feel like I have been to Florida. This ten-minute break is all I need.

Other days the cobwebs in my head are so thick ten minutes won't do the trick. Those are the days when it is important to have some other type of outlet. I work out. I jog, play tennis, or kick-box. There is nothing like punching and kicking a six-foot-tall plastic man in time to the beat of hard rock. After an intense kickboxing workout all the cobwebs seem to have disintegrated and I feel like a Charlie's Angel.

When Jacob was hospitalized, we didn't know whether or not Jacob would live much longer. Coping was not something I did very well over that period. I used to jog the eight kilometres down to the hospital for my shift with Jacob. Each step I took it felt like I was pushing a footprint deep into the sidewalk. Tears would stream down my cheeks and my arms would flail as I punch out the air. I must have looked ridiculous. But it didn't matter. By the time I reached the Hospital for Sick Children, I felt better. I could be the mother that I needed to be for Jacob and handle the difficult decisions. I was ready to hold him until tomorrow.

Make Someone Else Feel Special

When I am feeling low, I do something nice for someone else and I feel better. Making someone's day is one of the best feelings there is.

Every Friday I make a Jewish sweet bread called challah. Every Friday night, Jeff sits Jacob on his lap and they cut the bread together. We all say our prayers, and thank God for everything that he has given us. Jacob loves Fridays.

There are as many recipes for challah as there are Jewish cooks and cookbooks. A friend of mine shared her secret recipe with me. It consists of a little bit of this and a little bit of that. Each Friday I make four challahs. We keep one for our family, and I always give two or three away. Only special people receive our special challahs and the expressions on their faces as they open their door and see me standing there with a warm loaf in my arms is indescribable. I had thought about how special they were to me when I was making the challahs that morning and again when I delivered it in the afternoon. I made someone feel special, and that feeling made me feel so good inside.

Sometimes I just lay in bed wondering about whom I can make a challah for. Whom am I going to make smile? Somehow if I can make someone else smile I feel much better about myself.

Jacob has given me a gift. Without him, I really don't know if I would have truly appreciated the small kind gestures from others.

Smile

Sometimes it seems impossible to smile and people always ask me, "Ellen, why are you always smiling? How do you do it?" I have many reasons to smile. Wonderful family and friends surround me and the sound of Beverly and Ben playing and laughing surround Jacob.

He loves being surrounded by people and voices he recognizes and whenever I look at Jacob he is smiling. It's the little sounds that make him laugh: a spoon dropping on a ceramic tile, a nose being blown, a coughing fit from someone.

At the age of eight, Jacob is completely immobile. He isn't able to see the beauty that surrounds him. He is tube-fed for nutrition. He has to be suctioned because he can't control his secretions. Jacob has been through more in his brief eight years than most people will endure in a lifetime. And he smiles.

He isn't able to tell us his desires or his needs in words. Without words or explanations, Jacob has taught me. Jacob didn't only open my eyes, he opened my world.

My son faces each day and obstacle with courage, laughter and an inner strength. I have been blessed with a gift. Jacob has taught me to take a situation, any situation, and make it positive. He has taught me to accept life for what it is, and accept people for who they are. Jacob constantly reminds us of life's importance. He puts everything into perspective. Jacob can't speak, yet his message is loud and clear. He cannot see, but he has such a vision.

Epilogue

IT IS NOW 12:01 AM ON MAY 17, 2006.

Jacob is nine.

The house is silent except for the buzz of the refrigerator and the whir of Jacob's nutrition pump.

Everyone is in bed, fast asleep. It's my turn to wake up with the children. It's my turn to get up with Jacob in the middle of the night. Jeff sleeps. Beverly sleeps. Benjamin sleeps. All I know is that in six hours, when the house becomes alive again, another day will begin. Today he is nine. Thank goodness! Jacob's lessons continue on.

I love Holland!

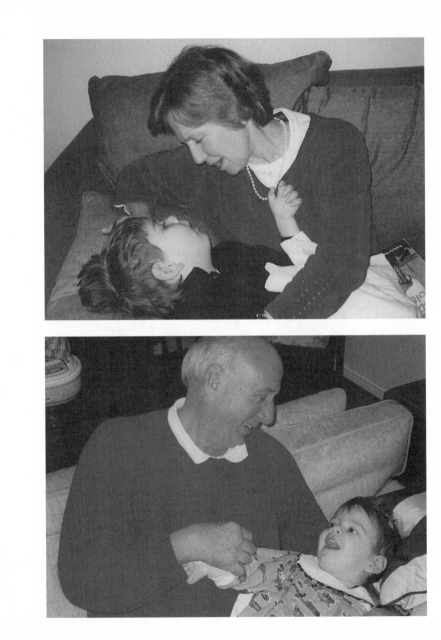

Jacob with his grandparents.

Acknowledgements

THANK GOODNESS FOR MY UNDERSTANDING AND loving network of friends and family, because without you this book would not be possible.

There are so many people to thank in so many different ways, yet you are all so important in the creation of *Lessons from Jacob*.

Edward Trapunski, my mentor into the world of literature and friend. If it weren't for Edward, this book would still be developing in my brain, instead of on paper. Jeff and I were invited to a fundraiser for the Juvenile Diabetes Research Foundation. We started bidding on a ghost writer for an article as one of the items in the silent auction. We won. I met with Edward one week later. We sat in Starbucks and I told him my idea about sharing all of the lessons that Jacob had taught me and everyone around us. He loved the idea, and through his guidance we put together a book proposal. Edward has continued to mentor me through this whole process. Edward, thank you for your guidance, wisdom and honesty.

Robert Mackwood, my agent and believer. From our first

meeting, Robert, from Seventh Avenue Literary Agency, loved this project. He informed me that he just had to find the right publishing company, who believed in our book. Through his persistence and dedication Robert merged *Lessons* together with Key Porter Books. Thank you, Robert, for your insight, your vision, and your friendship.

To Jordan Fenn, Jonathan Schmidt, Sheila Evely, Martin Gould, Carol Harrison, Jessica Yared, and the incredible talented people at Key Porter Books. Without you, this book would just be hundreds of eight-and-a-half-by-eleven sheets of paper, looking for a cover and a home. Jacob's story touched Jordan's heart right from the beginning. Thank you, Jordan, for your attachment to Jacob's story and perusing your gut feeling. Jonathan, your wisdom and knowledge are extremely fresh and inspiring. Robert was right: this company is the perfect home for *Lessons*. Thank you.

To Marla and Bob Gagne. Thank you for being there at our lowest moment. You completely empathized with us and made us realize we weren't alone.

To our special friends who help us run Jacob's Ladder— Jessica Palmer and Nora Glass—our wonderful board of directors and advisors, our dedicated and devoted committee members, and all of our incredible sponsors and volunteers: Jacob's life has been given further purpose because of all of you. Thank you for your continued support, heartfelt encouragement, and passion. You have helped us turn an extremely small charity into a million-dollar foundation that is making a huge mark in this world. Thank you for contributing to Jacob's legacy.

To Kayla Goren, Queenie, and Inge Spindel, Jacob's very special friends. Kayla, you opened Jacob's eyes to music, and our eyes to the reciprocal friendship between the two of you. That very special day in the hospital, I saw you reach Jacob's inner soul and bring him back to us. Your musical gift has touched Jacob's life and the two of you have such an intense bond. Queenie, the support you have given to Jacob's Ladder and our family is remarkable. Inge, your creative brilliance and passion has taken Jacob's Ladder to a level we never would have dreamed possible. You have taken Jacob's message and spread the word. You are all unbelievable, and I feel honoured to know all three of you.

Without Jacob's tireless team of pediatricians, Jacob wouldn't be here to share all of his great lessons. Thank you, all of you for taking such care of our Jacob. Norman Saunders, you have not only helped Jacob beat the odds, you have been our medical mentor for eight years. Thank you for your love, your understanding, your friendship, and your incredible insight.

Jacob has been fortunate to have the most incredible teachers every year of his life. They have not only taught Jacob amazing lessons, but they have shown Jeff and me how to look outside of the box. Thank you to all Jacob's teachers at Play and Learn and Beverley School. You are all truly gifts sent from above.

Speaking of teachers, without my friends and fellow teachers at Eitz Chaim Schools, I wouldn't be able to do half the things that I seem to do. Sitting around that staff-room table has helped me through many tough times. Thank you for your compassion and friendship. You are all so special.

I am so blessed to have such loving and caring aunts and uncles, who consistently check in just to make sure that everything is okay. Thank you for helping out any time, any place. Just knowing that you are there makes each day brighter.

Without Jacob's caregivers, our home wouldn't run the way it does. Daily, you brighten Jacob's day, and ours. Thank you for your gentleness, your strength, your devotion, and the genuine love that you show Jacob, Beverly, and Ben.

To our siblings: Alan, Marla, Shelli, Heather, Gary, Nancy, Robbie, Jennifer, and Russell. Without your love and support in every way, both physically and emotionally, this book would not have been possible. You have all helped us in your own very special ways, whether it be just checking in, taking Beverly out, bringing in meals, taking Jacob for walks, or just being together. We wouldn't be able to do the things that we do without all of you in our lives.

To Jacob's cousins: Bryan, Melanie, Dylan, Max, Zachary, Cassie, Jamie, and Bennett. Thank you for accepting Jacob as Jacob. He is your cousin who loves you all very much. Without all of your hugs, kisses, songs, and sweetness, Jacob wouldn't be so responsive and happy around other children. You have made him realize that the sound of little voices is safe and wonderful. Jacob is so lucky to have such loving cousins. Thank you for including Jacob, and keep asking all of your bright questions.

To Aunt Lynn, Nana, and Bubby, three of the bravest, strongest women I know. Without your encouragement and constant re-enforcement and belief that I can do anything, I don't know if I would have had the courage to write all my thoughts down. Thank you for always loving me no matter what.

To Mom and Dad. Words can't describe my life without both of you. You have given me the strength, determination, resilience, courage, and confidence to surprise even myself. Thank you for being tough when needed, and loving always. I can't even imagine the devastation you must have felt when you found out that your child's child was going to be so severely ill. Not only did you have to deal with your own pain, but also you had to guide me through mine. Jacob, Ben, and Beverly are so lucky to have you as grandparents, and I am grateful that I was chosen to be your daughter. Thank you for reading every excerpt that I sent to you while writing this book. Your encouraging comments kept me going until completion. I love you both so much.

To Ben and Beverly. I can't imagine life without both of you. You keep our household alive and laughing even at the toughest times. You both make your brother so proud. He loves to be around you, and his eyes light up when either of you enter a room. Every night when you both kiss Jacob goodnight, my heart melts. Beverly, you are so proud of your brother, and all that he has done. I am so proud of you. I will always remember that day when you were eighteen months of age and I came home from the hospital at 11 AM to try to catch some sleep. Watching you take those first steps to greet me at the door, was one of the most remarkable moments of my life. I hugged you and never wanted to let you go. You showed me that no matter how tough life can be, it still goes on, and every moment counts. Beverly and Ben, watching both of you achieve all of your milestones has given your father and me such happiness and joy.

Jeff, you are my partner, my best friend, and my love. Without your encouragement this book would not have happened. Thank you for all of those evenings, when you catered to the kids so that I could write. There were times when I wanted to call it quits, and you kept reminding me what an important job this was for me. You reminded me, how cathartic all of it was. Watching you with Jacob can bring tears to anyone's eyes. I can't imagine a better father. The way you look at him, the way you play with him, and the way you talk about him is truly heartfelt and inspiring. There is nothing that you wouldn't do for any of us. Thank you for sharing this road with me. I love you!

Jacob...all of this is for you, buddy. Because of you, the world is a better place. Jacob, you are a gift. I will cherish you always. Thank you for loving us, accepting us, forgiving us, and teaching us. I know that your Jacob's Ladder will climb to unimaginable heights. We just have to take it one rung at a time and enjoy every step.